LE MANS

A POCKET HISTORY
by DAVID BLUMLEIN

Transport Bookman
Publications Ltd

This book is not authorised or connected with the
Automobile Club de l'Ouest in any way.

All photographs are by kind permission
of the L.A.T. Photographic Archive

Distributed by Transport Bookman Publications Ltd,
8, South Street, Isleworth, Middlesex TW7 7DH, England

Printed in England by Wizard Printing Limited

085184 068-X

Foreward

Despite having 'done' the Le Mans 24-Hour race at various intervals for many years, it was not until the time in the 1990s, when I first accepted David Blumlein's offer to attend the race in his company, that I began to appreciate the depth of history and significance that the annual pageant represents.

Whilst previously I'd attended as a normal race-goer, admittedly sometimes to watch family friends like Graham Hill or my nephew Tim in a variety of machinery or friends like Nick Mason in with a chance of winning outright, I had never looked upon the 24 Hours as anything other than just another race. Longer perhaps and with a classier field and demanding endurance from the spectator as well as driver and crews. But it was still just a race.

Attending with David, who is *the* Le Mans history guru par excellence, however, opened my eyes for the first time to the great tradition, to the wonderful exploits of the past, to the vital part the race has played in the history of the development of the motor car itself.

Now you, dear reader, are, through the pages of this book, going to have the opportunity to attend Le Mans with David. You are very fortunate because you could not be in better hands. No one is better suited to guide you through what is without doubt the world's finest motor racing spectacle and to give you a unique and priceless additional ingredient - added value!

Enjoy and bonne chance . . . .

Brian Harvey
30 August 2002

Preface

The basis of this book is a series of articles I wrote as a brief history of the Le Mans 24-hour race for "Four Small Wheels". This is Grand Prix Model's specialist magazine and the Editor, Brian Harvey, engaged me, as a regular contributor, to produce this work in celebration of the 60th running of the world-famous race. I have since added further material to update the story and have included a reference section which highlights the points of special interest in each of the separate races.

In choosing the pictures, I have resisted the temptation to show primarily the overall winners (although some are included) but rather have sought to convey something of the character of the race with its multi-varied participants and its changing setting over the years.

Should this book awaken an interest and render the reader hungry for more knowledge of this great French institution, I shall be well rewarded.

D.A.P.B.

Acknowledgments

This book would never have been conceived were it not for the opportunities to put pen to paper afforded to me by my good friends at Grand Prix Models, Brian and Rachel Harvey, André Marot and Mark Chitty. They have and still do invite me to write about Le Mans and this has forged over the years a solid basis from which I have been able to build. Furthermore, Brian has generously seized every opportunity to engineer the opening of doors into Le Mans, furnishing me with insights of which most enthusiasts can only dream.

The book would never have reached reality without the devoted services of Elena Deer who has at all times enthusiastically worked away at converting my 19th century manuscript techniques into a 21st century level of acceptability. Her patience while I decided to change this and that was unsurpassed as was her reassurance that all could be accomplished so easily and, thanks to her proficiency, was!

Clive Stroud of Chater & Scott responded with genuine encouragement from the start and so kindly and willingly proffered his professional support and guidance, steering me in the right direction to get the whole project off the ground and undertaking to set up the publishing process.

I received the warmest of welcomes from the LAT Photographic Archive where Tim Wright, Kevin Wood, James Roberts and their colleagues extended such kindness and trust in me that I was able to make full use of their superb facilities as if I were one of their professional team!

Nathan Lauder of "Fibre" made artistic sense of my almost incomprehensible instructions to produce the up-to-date circuit diagram featuring the different changes over the years.

And to act as "protection" to my work I was privileged to have the services of Graham Turner, several of whose original Le Mans paintings adorn my home.

Finally, a life-long motoring enthusiast friend, Robert Rowland, very kindly undertook to proof-read the full manuscript with his usual meticulous care.

Nothing worthwhile is ever achieved single-handedly in this world and I have been blessed with these good people whom I thank most sincerely for all they have done to help me create this work.

David Blumlein
Ealing, September 2002

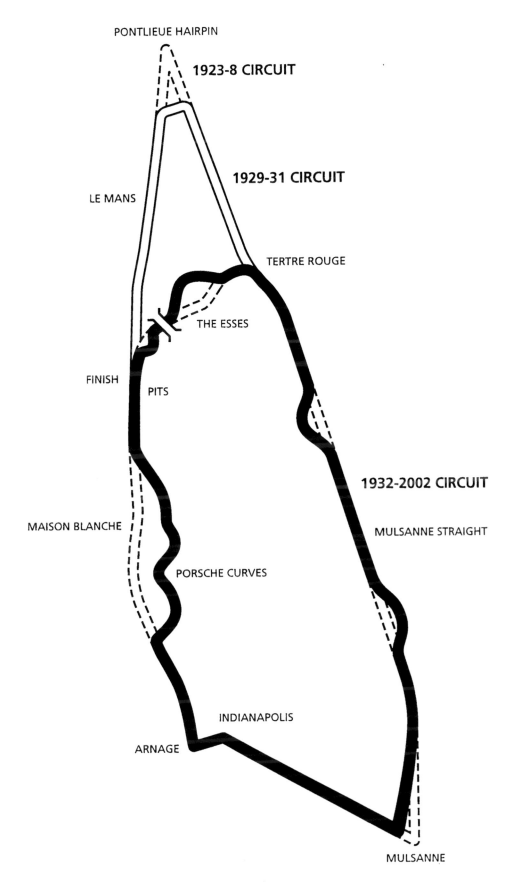

PONTLIEUE HAIRPIN

1923-8 CIRCUIT

1929-31 CIRCUIT

LE MANS

TERTRE ROUGE

THE ESSES

FINISH

PITS

1932-2002 CIRCUIT

MAISON BLANCHE

MULSANNE STRAIGHT

PORSCHE CURVES

INDIANAPOLIS

ARNAGE

MULSANNE

Contents

Chapter 1

Introduction

The city of Le Mans, capital of the Department of Sarthe, has been no stranger either to history or to the motor car, or indeed a happy combination of the two. The English have long had links with this city: go to see the cathedral of St Julien for there took place the marriage of Matilda and Geoffrey Plantagenet who ushered in our famous dynasty and it was here in 1133 that was born one of our more capable monarchs, Henry II. Thus Le Mans was in the English blood from early on and our countrymen did not finally let go of the city until 1447 in the twilight of the Hundred Years' War. More recently there was a Battle of Le Mans when in 1871 the Germans defeated the French during the Franco-Prussian conflict, and of course they did it again in 1940. Fittingly, 1927 Bentley winner Sammy Davis was among those who helped to liberate the city in 1944.

The car came early to Le Mans too, thanks to the Bollée family. Amédée senior had a steam carriage on the road by 1873 and once son Léon had launched his effective petrol-driven Voiturette, car manufacturing grew in Le Mans. Even William Morris cashed in, buying in 1924 the Léon Bollée works, located at Les Sablons in the east of the city, in an attempt to tap the French market from within. His Morris-Léon Bollée cars were conspicuously unsuccessful but at least his works patriotically provided facilities for the visiting Bentley team in those years! And Renault broke out from Billancourt for the first time and came to Le Mans in 1936; they are still there, helping to keep the city a true home of motoring.

Not surprisingly such early associations with the new-fangled motor car stirred local enthusiasm for sporting activities. The Automobile Club de la Sarthe, the forerunner of the A.C.O.(Automobile Club de l' Ouest), was formed as early as October 1905 and the first real Grand Prix, the 1906 French Grand Prix, was run on a 64-mile circuit to the east of Le Mans, thus establishing a racing tradition which has outshone all others. Another Grand Prix was held in 1911, this time on a 35-mile triangular circuit to the south of the city; it was important because it incorporated parts of the present day circuit. Other races were held in 1912 and 1913 together with cycle-car events but it was not until after the Great War that the Circuit Permanent de la Sarthe, basically as we know it, was established. The most important event held on this layout prior to the 24-hour race was the 1921 French Grand Prix won by Jimmy Murphy's Duesenberg, by no means the last time the Americans were to make their presence felt at the Sarthe!

What a mighty inspiration descended on the three founder figures, Georges Durand, Charles Faroux and Emile Coquille who together conceived the idea of a major race at Le Mans for production cars, to demonstrate their reliability through twenty-four hours! Severe regulations were devised, the main requirements being that entries were to be catalogued touring cars with all the necessary road equipment and four seats except for cars under 1100 c.c. which had to have two seats. Minimum distances according to engine size were laid down and there was to be no outright winner as such; cars would qualify for the Rudge Whitworth Triennial Cup.

Eighteen manufacturers accepted the challenge for that first event in 1923. A Spring date (26-27 May) was chosen in the hope of favourable weather but as it turned out squalls of wind and rain greeted the start and compounded competitors' problems all through the night. Army searchlights helped to illuminate the dangerous corners and, despite the organisation being inevitably primitive to start with, a large crowd turned out for what was a novelty in Europe (although many twenty-four hour races had been held in artificial conditions in America previously).

Perhaps not unexpectedly the entry was almost entirely French, foreigners being two Belgian Excelsiors (5.3-litres), a 3-litre Bentley and the Montier Special based on a Model T Ford. Two 3-litre Chenard et Walckers actually completed the greatest distance followed by two 2-litre Bignans, with the Bentley and an Excelsior tieing for fifth "place". But the surprising outcome was that, of the thirty-three starters, only three failed to finish, a S.A.R.A. having the doubtful distinction of being the first car ever to retire in the history of the race! And modern motorists will notice that of those eighteen marques, only Bentley survives today, albeit under German control.

Chapter 2

1924 - 1930 The Rise of Bentley

If the first running of the 24-hour race had been a success, the choice of date most certainly was not and the traditional mid-June weekend, offering longer daylight (and hopefully more sunshine) was settled upon for the 1924 event.

Already the "Grand Prix d'Endurance" was growing up. Tougher regulations included the need for cars to stop after five laps to erect hoods which then had to be worn for twenty laps, and only after minimum intervals of twenty laps could fuel, oil or water be replenished. Furthermore, the A.C.O. wisely started to provide fairground style entertainment to keep the many spectators amused over the twenty-four hours. It all helped Le Mans to acquire quickly a status superior to its rivals.

That lone Bentley of Duff and Clement returned, the sole foreign intruder amidst an array of thirty-nine French runners. Formidable opposition came from Chenard et Walcker, 3-litre Bignans, a 3.2 Aries and the fine 3.4 six-cylinder Lorraines. In the early stages the big 4-litre straight-eight Chenard set the pace but this car soon caught fire at Pontlieue and was burned out. Indeed most of the French opposition faded by midnight, leaving the Bentley to tackle the Lorraines which it did successfully, giving the marque the first of five wins. This success sparked off enthusiasm chez Bentley for the event and accounts for their serious support during the remaining years of the decade. And the weather did stay dry and sunny which resulted in only 14 cars finishing!

By 1925 we can say that the race came of age internationally for the 49 starters now included seven Italians, six British (including, yes, an Austin Seven) and, most welcome, an American entry from Chrysler. This was the year of the inauguration of the famous Le Mans-type start and, for this year only, the pits were sited on the Mulsanne Straight while a dispute with a local landowner was resolved; henceforth they would resort to their familiar location at Raineries on the western side of the circuit. Hoods up first thing was also a modified rule and the effect of this eliminated the works Bentley which promptly ran out of fuel when fighting the 3-litre Sunbeams. One of the Wolverhampton cars finished second with a cracked chassis, the only British survivor, but it was the stamina of the Lorraine that brought the French car the first of two wins. Nor must we overlook the achievement of the little 1100 c.c. Chenard et Walcker 'tanks' which won the Triennial and Biennial Cups.

The absence of any Chenard et Walcker in 1926 ominously presaged the decline of the French challenge for the outright winner (an honour whose existence was not acknowledged until 1928). An exception was Peugeot which made a first appearance with two 3.8-litre sleeve valve cars but luck was against them (one was disqualified!) as indeed it was against the Bentleys which probably suffered more than anything from inadequate preparation owing to preoccupation with record-breaking. More Americans came in the form of a Willys-Knight and two Overland Sixes but their efforts were never a serious threat and Lorraine survived to take the first three places, the last French win until 1937! But, alas, that was enough for them as well and the marque only ever reappeared in private hands. An innovation had been the Index of Performance category, a formula based on the actual distance travelled in relation to a minimum required distance. To become so much the preserve of the little French cars in the post-war years, this first Index prize was won by the powerful 2-litre side valve O.M.

As we look back, it was the next four years that came to be thought of as Bentley's Golden Age, a period during which British support for and success at Le Mans became an important and integral part of this wonderful race's character and history. If in 1927 the entries were unexpectedly low (22 starters) Lady Fate had reserved a very special drama to compensate, for it was to go down as one of history's most remarkable races! The scene was the corner at the Maison Blanche (White House), the cause a 2-litre Th. Schneider which had skidded, blocking the road. Callingham with the new 4.5-litre Bentley arrived next, rolling over; then another Th. Schneider and Duller's 3-litre Bentley joined in; add an 1100 c.c. Aries and finally Sammy Davis in the third Bentley; a monumental pile-up with five cars totally wrecked from which Davis managed to extract his car with a bent frame and front axle! But the Bentley got back in the race and when the leading big Aries cried enough towards the end, Davis and Benjafield found themselves the winners. Two little 1100 c.c. Salmsons were next home perhaps hoping for an even more unexpected result but they took the Index and the Biennial Cup all the same.

A year later British involvement increased, no doubt prompted by Bentley's sensational win, and Lagonda, Aston Martin and Alvis appeared, the latter with front-wheel drive to keep the French Tractas company. However, it was the Americans now rather than the French who provided the serious opposition; a big straight-eight Stutz and four Chrysler 72s, the French languishing almost entirely in the sub 2-litre classes. It turned out to be an Anglo-American battle which was in doubt to the end and certainly the finest race so far. Brisson's Stutz had led for much of the night and Barnato's Bentley only moved ahead when the American car lost some gears on the Sunday afternoon. But the British car was itself in trouble as well with a cracked chassis and only just made it home, Woolf Barnato whose money kept Bentley afloat starting a hat-trick of wins. And those Americans came home second, third and fourth.

In 1929 for the first time the circuit had been modified as a safety measure. The dangerous Pontlieue hairpin was cut off by a new link road, but still in the suburbs of Le Mans. Bentley faced the trans-Atlantic challenge. But the experience of six Le Mans races paid handsome dividends as the Americans fell back; Bentley filled the first four places and we had to wait nearly thirty years for Jaguar to emulate the same feat. Furthermore, the Speed Six also clinched the Index, the largest car to do so.

Thus the stage was set for Bentley's last triumph but with a change of the leading cast: the big white 7.1-litre Mercedes of Carraciola and Werner. Charles Faroux, one of the race's founders, was moved by the British successes to launch a blistering attack on the failure of the French manufacturers to produce Le Mans winners but his words fell on too many deaf ears: only three French cars, a Bugatti (with the first all-female crew) and two Tractas, all in the small categories, ran in 1930. In fact that year recorded the smallest number of starters ever - only 17. By the end of the decade the race had become a public showground for foreign makes to earn world-wide publicity.

Supercharged Bentleys (despite W.O.'s disapproval) supplemented the works car and, although lacking reliability, they helped destroy the Teutonic opposition which failed during the night. It was another British triumph with Bentleys first and second, the Roesch Talbot third (and taking the Index), Lea-Francis winning the 1.5 litre class (for the second time) and Birkin topping it all with a lap record.

It was an amazing climax, but economic recession lay in the background and within a year Bentley had become just another victim. It was truly the end of an era, but the Le Mans 24-hour race was here to stay!

The first start in 1923, Belgian Excelsiors lead Lorraines, the Bentley and winning Chenard et Walckers

Front - Drive Alvis leads Aston-Martin and Front-Drive Tracta in 1928

Mulsanne in 1928. Itala passes Lagonda in famous sand-pit!

Bentley Speed Six closes the marque's golden era with a win - 1930.

1931 - the winning Alfa-Romeo at Pontlieue.

French Sports Cars

Two-stroke Tracta chases air-cooled S.A.R.A. at the modified Pontlieue corner in 1929

Class-winning Caban Special enters Pontlieue in 1929

Bugatti Type 37 leads rare Citroën in the new "Esses" in 1932

The changing face of sports cars – Delage Coupé winning Bugatti and Adlers show the way forward in 1937.

Last pre-war race – Morgan 4.4 hounded by V-12 Lagonda in 1939

Chapter 3

1931 - 1935 Italian Superiority - Part 1

Exit works Bentley, backstage France, enter Italy. The star: Alfa-Romeo, or more specifically the 8C 2300. This superb machine merits a few background words for it becomes very quickly the dominating car in sports-car racing in the early thirties and mopped up Le Mans for four years running.

Vittorio Jano's 1500 and 1750 six-cylinder Alfas already had three Mille Miglia triumphs to their credit when the great designer was first working on the new eight cylinder version. Indeed, a 1750 six-cylinder, driven by Earl Howe and Callingham, finished fifth at Le Mans in 1930 on the marque's first appearance while the Bentleys were reaching the climax of their wonderful contribution to the race's history. The 8C 2300, with cylinders in two blocks of four with the twin camshaft drive taken off the centre of the crankshaft, first appeared in 1931 and soon became practically invincible.

Thus do we find two of the longer wheelbase versions, as demanded by the regulations, as serious contenders for the 1931 Le Mans race. The opposition came mainly from three works Type 50 4.9-litre Bugattis painted in a threatening black, weighing almost two tons and surely laying claim to being 'even faster lorries in the world'! - (Bugatti had once dismissed the Le Mans Bentleys as 'lorries'). Bentley, Lorraine, Stutz and Mercedes were there but only as private entries and Britain enhanced the entry by providing some 3-litre Talbots, 1.5-litre Aston Martins and 750 c.c. MGs. Two Chryslers might have threatened the scarlet red Alfas while the only support France could muster for the huge Bugattis was a collection of worthy tiddlers.

The drama of the race centred around the Michelin tyre failures of the heavy Bugattis. Early in the race Chiron's car threw a tread but worst of all Maurice Rost's car had a tyre wrap itself around a brake drum in the early evening, causing a horrific crash in which an imprudent spectator was killed and Rost sorely injured. When Chiron's car repeated the tread throwing act once more, Jean Bugatti wisely withdrew the remaining cars. This left Alfa Romeo in charge and once the Zehender/Marinoni car had crashed, Birkin and Howe took a lead they were never to lose. It was Italy's first triumph in the race and only six cars were classified at the end, among them a Talbot in third behind the Mercedes and Bertelli's Aston Martin winning the 1.5-litre class which was to become almost entirely the marque's property at Le Mans in the first half of the decade.

1932 heralded a further revision to the circuit: out went the Pontlieue section altogether. The A.C.O. had sensibly decided to build on its own land a link between the pits and the Mulsanne Straight which henceforth incorporated what we now know as the Esses, affording splendid spectator viewing and reducing the lap to 8.3 miles, but still adequately long for a full field to spread out over twenty-four hours. The village was being built up at this time as well.

As far as the race was concerned, anybody who harboured any thoughts about winning outright now had to have an Alfa 2300! There were six on the entry list that year including the works machines. To attempt to displace them were Type 55 Bugattis and privately driven Mercedes, Stutz and a blower Bentley, but on paper the Alfas were the only likely winners. What could not have been foreseen was another in the series of incidents at White House! On the very first lap Trevoux overturned the Bentley and there was a certain amount of difficulty in moving the car out of harm's way. A little later Minoia's works Alfa arrived at the corner a shade too fast, spun in the restricted space and crashed. The Italian had previously just overtaken Brisson's Stutz which then arrived around the corner to find the red car spinning in his path. The French driver inevitably crashed. Despite flag warnings to stop, drivers carried on and Marinoni, endeavouring to make up lost time, overtook a slower car into the bend, put his offside wheels on the grass and went broadside on, the tail of his Alfa smiting an projecting portion of the Bentley; a total of four cars wrecked at White House!

Retirements left Raymond Sommer and Cortese's works Alfas on top, the Italian's car suffering from parts falling off! The Frenchman, in only his second Le Mans, had decided before the season to purchase an Alfa 2300 and came into possession of the car which was used as a demonstrator at the 1931 Paris Salon. Aerodynamic modifications were made by his friend Figoni, not yet well-known as a coachbuilder, and this car went on to win with co-driver Chinetti ill for most of the race, leaving Sommer to do the lion's share of the driving.

No wonder Nuvolari was happy to share Sommer's car the following year on his only appearance at Le Mans. The 'Flying Mantuan' was to win but not without real excitement. Five of the indispensable Alfa Romeos were lined up against a 6.9 Duesenberg and some old stagers such as a Bentley, Lorraine and 4.9 Bugatti. Plenty of small British cars joined in, new runners including Rileys and a Singer while the French continued to stay backstage with a host of 'petites cylindrées'. Fiery drama struck early on the Sunday morning when Mme Siko's 1750 Alfa crashed, cut down three trees and burned vigorously but the race had become a straight fight between Nuvolari/Sommer, Chinetti/Varent and Chiron/Cortese on the eight-cylinder Alfas. For Nuvolari troubles began on the Sunday morning when a leaking fuel tank had to be plugged. In the meantime Cortese overturned his car, leaving Chinetti to challenge Nuvolari who, with characteristic skill, had regained the lead from the Chinetti/Varent car.

The last hour was pure theatre: Nuvolari was two minutes ahead at three o'clock with a worsening fuel leak which much chewing-gum had failed to stem. A quarter past three: Varent was in the lead but Nuvolari passed again. With eight minutes to go Chinetti, who had taken over from Varent, passed a stationary Nuvolari in the pits. Nuvolari rejoined and on the last lap the lead changed thrice; when Chinetti made an error at Arnage, Nuvolari slipped through to win by some ten seconds! Alfa Romeo first, second and third but, just as Bentley failed at the height of its glory, the Alfa works team was to be withdrawn for financial reasons. The little Riley came fourth, snapping up the Index of Performance, the little Singer thirteenth and last.

Good Le Mans cars have a habit of staying competitive for several years and there was still life in Jano's 8C 2300 yet. Improved double storey pits were ready for 1934 and the race attracted forty-four starters, over half of which were British mostly in the smaller capacity classes. No Milanese works cars of course, but four privately entered Alfa Romeos provided the favourites. Sommer's car, early in the lead, caught fire after only two hours, two more Alfas failed, and by the Sunday morning Chinetti and Etancelin seemed to have the race in their pockets if they could keep going. Older rivals such as Bugattis and even Lorraine fell out or back and it was a shoal of smaller British cars that threatened the leader. In fact, Riley had a field day, their six cars all finishing, the best in second and third positions overall, rather reminiscent of the Salmsons in 1927!

Bentley had won the race five times; now Alfa Romeo had won four times. Success once more seemed quite possible, there being no obvious challenger to the Italian car in the big league. Four private entrants of the Alfas led the huge field of fifty-eight runners in 1935 and quietly fought among themselves for the lead, but retirements reduced their number to one, just as in 1934, and it was the red Meadows-engined Lagonda of Hindmarsh and Fontes that overtook the Stoffel/Dreyfus Alfa on Sunday morning. But the big British car started to drop back with failing oil pressure and only a confusion in the Alfa pit allowed the Lagonda to survive long enough to win - a very unexpected result, but once again a Le Mans win did not guarantee commercial survival: Lagonda was in financial trouble! The large British contingent did well in that rather wet race, with Aston Martin coming third, winning the Index and Biennial Cup, a resounding final success in the Bertelli chapter.

And so the superb Alfa Romeo 8C 2300 was not destined to win again, and the company, although a front-runner during several appearances in the post-war races, has yet to emulate its performance at the Sarthe circuit in the early thirties, for it was this period that really clinched the magic of the Alfa Romeo name. Furthermore, Le Mans had itself by now become so prestigious a race that manufacturers were over-anxious to participate; a mere dozen years after that pioneering first event. Le Mans was now the most important race in the motor sport calendar. Very few sporting cars had not already joined in at some stage and at some level.

Chapter 4

1937 - 1939 French Revival

France was in much political turmoil by mid-1936, the characteristic instability of successive governments of the Third Republic and the divided nature of the political scene being especially apparent after the April elections that year. By June strikes had paralysed industry and workers had occupied factories. The agreement forged at the Hotel Matignon by which most demands of the workforce were met came too late to save that year's race, cancellation coming a mere week before its scheduled date. This caused enormous cost not only to the A.C.O. but to the sixty entrants which had intended to take part. Welcome French entries had come from Delage, Delahaye and Talbot; two Alfa-Romeos were to have appeared, while Britain was sending her usual strong contingent: Aston Martin (with the new 2-litre Speed Model), a team of Austin Sevens, Riley and Frazer-Nash; Germany's Adler was due and the whole cast was supported by many private entries.

This disappointment nevertheless forms something of a natural break in the story of the 24-Hours. Two considerations spring to mind. First, there was a resurgence of interest by the French in sports-car racing. This can be explained chiefly by the advent of the 750 kg Grand Prix formula introduced for the 1934 season. It prompted the massive Nazi-subsidised effort of the Mercedes and Auto-Union teams to dominate Grand Prix racing so as to emphasise the superiority of Germany. France of course could not hope to keep up, its best contender, the Bugatti type 59, being hopelessly outclassed from the outset. And so France started organising its major races for sports cars; the 1936 French G.P. and the G.P. de Marne at Reims were typical examples. French manufacturers responded and soon the 'tank' Bugatti 57 was competing with the Delahaye 135 and the Talbot 150C.

Secondly, we can see definite technical progress in the sports cars of the late thirties over their counterparts up to 1935. Until this date the successful sports cars were really more refined versions of traditional vintage concepts, sturdy in construction with firm suspension by semi-elliptic springs. But by the middle of the decade there was a trend towards the use of independent suspension for better road-holding and genuine attempts to utilise streamlining to increase performance. The BMW 328 which appeared in 1936 and the Alfa Romeo 2900 were shining examples of this new breed of sports car.

These developments were much in evidence at Le Mans in 1937 especially since by then the regulations were only demanding that all the cars should have two comfortable front facing seats, rear seats being optional. And so, what did the spectators see lined up in echelon before the pits? Plenty of evidence of the French revival: the Bugatti works were back with two 'tank' T57G streamliners, seven Delahaye 135s, two Talbot 150Cs, three Darl'mat Peugeot sports, (302 chassis, 402 engines and Paulin designed bodies), a 3-litre Delage coupe, private Bugattis, Gordini's Simcas, and even two Chenard et Walcker 'tanks' revived from the mid-twenties - a veritable sea of blue (except that the Delage was painted in an orangey red!). Ranged against these were Sommer in an Alfa Romeo 2900, a 4.5-litre Lagonda, BMW 328s, German Adlers, and the now usual host of smaller-engined British cars including an H.R.G., official Austin Sevens, private Singers and an unlikely Ford Ten!

And the technical progress was equally apparent: independent springing on the Delahayes, Talbots, Delage and Peugeots (which also used Cotal gearboxes), on the German entries and the advanced Alfa Romeo; streamlined bodies on the works Bugattis, Peugeots and above all on the three Adlers whose aerodynamic efficiency seemed to compensate for their humble side-valve engines. Le Mans 1937 reflected a major step forward in the design of the modern sporting car.

The race itself (started by John Cobb, the world 24-Hour record holder) was quickly resolved. Sommer, having led for the first few laps in the potent Alfa Romeo, soon retired after handing over the lead to the Wimille-Benoist Bugatti which easily stayed there for the remaining twenty three and a half hours, their distance of 2,043 miles at an average speed of 85 m.p.h. comfortably breaking the 1933 records.

It was in those early laps also that disaster struck, once again down by White House, but this time with tragic results. Rene Kippeurt, a garage owner from Sevres and a relatively inexperienced amateur, lost control of his old Bugatti coming out of the notorious bends ahead of a high-speed bunch of cars, his car ploughing into Roth's BMW and thus blocking the track. The slight kink in the road and the high hedge on the right helped to unsight his pursuers who unavoidably slammed into the wreckage, Tremoulet's Delahaye, Pat Fairfield's Frazer-Nash BMW, the Talbot of 'Ralph' (Raphael de las Casas) and Forestier's Riley. Kippeurt was killed outright while the blameless Fairfield, one of Britain's most respected drivers, survived only until the Monday morning, Forestier being the sole driver to escape injury. Fortunately, others following were alerted in time but the wreckage of Kippeurt's and Tremoulet's cars could not be completely removed and lined the track for the rest of the race, lamps being rested on top of each to remind drivers in the darkness.

As the race went on the French domination at the front remained intact and the Delahayes supported their leading compatriots to the end, Dreyfus putting up a monumental drive to third place after earlier delays with a damaged door that was judged to have contravened the regulations! The orange Delage ran reliably to fourth place, winning its class, as did two of the little Simcas and France's joy was completed by the winning Bugatti (its team-mate had unfortunately fallen by the wayside) scooping the Index of Performance as well. Loud did the 'Marseillaise' sound forth that year as Alsace had clearly taken turns with Lorraine, the previous French winner of some eleven years earlier!

In the 2-litre class Germany beat France for although all the Peugeots finished they were outpaced by the ultra-quiet Adler streamlined 'saloon'. Nor was Britain left out of the honours even though most of the smaller brigade did not survive. Aston Martin took yet again the 1500 c.c. class (and 5th place overall) and one of the 2-litre Speed Models won the Biennial Cup. And that unlikely Ford Ten did finish despite getting away with some monstrous rule bending; when it stopped during heavy rain out on the circuit, the team chief Jack Horsfall (of post-war Aston Martin fame) walked out to it, dried the electrics and drove it back to the pits where it resumed the race. Perhaps the French were too elated to be too harsh!

A year later, two big V-12 Delahayes, lined up at the head of the field, brought the concept of the sports-racing car much nearer, anticipating the prototype category which the A.C.O. questionably introduced for the post-war races. Le Mans was already moving away from the original raison d'être as a touring car race.

In 1938 the French remained formidable although there were surprisingly no Bugattis that year. In fact the home country provided no less than 28 of the 42 starters - five normal Delahaye 135s to back up the thinly disguised Grand Prix versions already mentioned, six Talbots (a 4.5-litre for Chinetti-Etancelin, three 4-litres and two Lago SS coupés), the previous year's Delage completely re-bodied, an Amilcar (once again), three up-graded Darl'mat Peugeots and no less than ten Simcas various. Ten mixed British of mainly vintage chassis including a four wheel Morgan, two more Adler streamlined saloons and two Alfa Romeos constituted the opposition.

It was one of the latter that turned the contest into France versus Italy. Sommer once again headed the trans-Alpine attack with a superb streamlined coupé by Touring on a 2900 chassis, the most sophisticated of sports machinery at that time. And when the 'Grand Prix Sprint' of the early laps was resolved with the big Delahayes dropping out, Sommer's Alfa took full command, stretching its lead unmercifully until it had an eleven lap advantage by three-quarters distance. The Delahaye 135s were the best of the rest and on the Chaboud-Tremoulet car hangs a tale: Chaboud had been a reluctant starter judging that the car had no real chance but Tremoulet, deprived of part of his ear in the 1937 pile-up, wanted to avenge his misfortune. When, however, the car was stuck in top gear during the night, their roles were reversed. Tremoulet had had enough but Chaboud, seeing his opponents wilting, now felt he had a chance. And carry on they did, in top gear for sixteen hours and when the Alfa finally broke on the Sunday afternoon, victory was theirs! Another Delahaye came second, underlining the strength of their lorry-based engines, followed by a 4-litre Talbot - a finish at last for the Lago inspired car. This year a sole surviving Peugeot beat the Adler in the 2-litre section, so France finally beat Germany while a French-entered Singer won the 1100 c.c. class. And all those Simcas? Well, one of the tiniest with only 568 c.c. won the increasingly important Index of Performance. What more could France ask?

There was to be no let up in the French effort and in 1939 the format of the entry list was rather similar except that Bugatti was back, this time with a supercharged 'tank' for Wimille and Veyron while Germany sent reinforcements for the one Adler in the shape of three BMWs, one a streamlined coupé. No more Darl' mat Peugeots in mid-field (hadn't honour been restored the year before?) but Britain sent, in addition to its usual contingent of smaller capacity cars, two V-12 Lagondas with torsion bar independent front suspension, the brain-child of W.O. Bentley, back after nearly a decade. Alfa Romeo produced only a 2.6-litre coupe for Sommer this time but in the race it misbehaved, allowing one of the two potent 3-litre Delages the centre-stage until it too suffered engine problems which slowed it down. The Bugatti was on hand to take over the lead which it held to the end and the Delage managed to keep second place ahead of the two clockwork-like Lagondas. BMW won the 2-litre class with the coupé and H.R.G. took over Aston Martin's role by winning the 1.5-litre category, making this almost a British preserve throughout the thirties. The Index? One of Gordini's Simca-based machines obliged for France yet again!

But storm clouds were gathering over Europe and thus our pre-war story ends. The international battles which had been so enjoyable on the track now took on an altogether more sinister character. France's Le Mans revival had been thorough but, alas, in direct contrast to her ability to overcome the most devastating threat to her security. The R.A.F. briefly and then the Luftwaffe took over the sacred track.

Chapter 5

1945 - 1959 Britain rises again

Like so much in France, the famous circuit bore a good deal of suffering during the Second World War. Before the collapse of France in 1940 the R.A.F. had used the airstrip adjacent to the pits straight but by the 18th June the first German invaders had reached the city of Le Mans. Their Luftwaffe quickly enlarged these airfield facilities to form a fighter base, even going so far as to use the Mulsanne Straight as a runway. The local railway network and the Renault factory to the south of the city naturally attracted the Allies' attention in 1943 and 1944 as did the big marshalling yard at Arnage, these air raids causing extensive damage for light losses on the part of the attackers. Just after D-Day all airfields in northern France became obvious priority targets and on the night of 9/10 June Le Mans duly received its share of the treatment. When the city was finally liberated on the 8th August 1944, the allied troops found the old circuit's grandstands just a skeleton with many of the other buildings gone - what had not been destroyed by the bombers was burned down by the retreating Germans. However, the footbridge across the track on the bend after the pits was still standing!

Much of the circuit resembled a lunar landscape with many of the trees, especially in the Mulsanne area where was established a camp for prisoners, having disappeared, but when the decision was taken in 1948 to hold the race again in the following year, much work was undertaken to restore the pits and grandstands and the track itself, basically unchanged, was completely resurfaced.

And so by June 1949 the scene was set for the celebrated race to make a come-back after an interval of ten years and we note one very significant modification to the rules: 'prototypes' were to be permitted, cars intended for production but which were not yet on sale to the public. This was prompted by the comparative lack of entries available in those austere years after the cessation of hostilities, but could the A.C.O. have realised what flood gates they were opening?

The starters for that first post-war race were numbered an encouraging 49 even though much of the front-running machinery had pre-war origins: lots of Delahayes, Delages and Talbots, a 1938 Derby-built Bentley (the streamlined Embiricos car already with 60,000 miles on the clock), private Singer, M.G., Alvis, Riley and Aston-Martin entries and the familiar assortment of small French cars, mostly Simca-based. But there were some exciting new cars as well, not least the 2-litre V-12 Ferraris, one of which in the hands of Chinetti and Selsdon was the ultimate winner, and the DB2 Aston Martin with Bentley-designed Lagonda engine - W.O. was still there! The field that year was also coloured by two Czech two-stroke Aero Minors, a 4 c.v. Renault, a Riley-engined

Healey saloon and the race's first diesel entry, a 4.4-litre Delettrez. A Frazer-Nash followed the second-placed Delage home and the Bentley came sixth, the owner thereafter resuming his continental tour! Surely that was the real Le Mans back again?

As the new decade unfolded the revival at Le Mans gathered momentum; there were some sixty starters for the 1950 race, thirty-three of them French of which twenty-five were of small capacities. If the half-dozen big contenders from France were fewer than usual, there was nevertheless plenty of evidence of increasing British strength - three XK120 Jaguars and DB2 Aston Martins and an Allard J2 with V8 Cadillac power. And there was an American revival too, for this race marked the start of Briggs Cunningham's devoted campaign to win the 24-Hours for the stars and stripes. He had brought along a Cadillac saloon and a strangely bodied open version dubbed 'Le Monstre' because of its lack of aesthetic appeal. Five Ferraris lined up after their unexpected success the previous year and other interesting entries came from such as Nash Healey, Jowett with their flat-four Jupiter, a Skoda, a second diesel, the M.A.P. (the first mid-engined car to run at Le Mans), and yet another pre-war Bentley (Hall's 1934 T.T. car) to keep its 1938 stable-mate company.

Raymond Sommer (twice a pre-war winner) dashed off into the lead with his blue Ferrari 195S but, as in 1937, not for long and the challenge revolved around the other Ferraris, the Talbot, Allard and Jaguar. Rosier, the French Champion, had his authority stamped on the race by nightfall and, when a rocker shaft needed changing on the Talbot at dawn, he had a six lap lead. Having let his son do a couple of laps while he himself consumed bananas as his one repast of the race, Rosier resumed a lap down on the Talbot of Guy Mairesse and Meyrat but quickly overhauled Hadley's Jaguar and then his compatriots to claim victory. The Jaguar's clutch gave up with three hours to go and the Allard finished third followed by the Nash-Healey and two Aston-Martins, the first of which won its class and shared the Index of Performance honours with a little Monopole-Panhard. British success was enhanced by Frazer-Nash and Jowett winning their categories.

It was, however, to be the last French victory for twenty-two years. This was partly the result of post-war French government policy that taxed large-engined cars ruthlessly while additionally giving little social support and materials to labour intensive companies which did not turn out plenty of cheaper cars for the nation's immediate needs. Delahaye, Delage and Talbot were effectively killed off and the roads of France were filled with the buzz of small capacity engines such as the 4 c.v. Renault and the Panhard flat-twin. It was the latter engine especially, usually mounted in Monopole or D.B. chassis, which remarkably gave the French a share of the spoils at Le Mans in the fifties and early sixties by its near monopoly of the organiser's darling, the Index of Performance.

At this point the Le Mans race can be said to have entered a golden age. Manufacturers were now getting back into their stride and competition for the lucrative markets especially across the Atlantic was becoming intense. The best stage in the world which demonstrated the reliable speed of a motor car was seen to be the 24-Hours race whose prestige far surpassed that of every rival. To win at Le Mans, then as now, meant much more than all other competition successes put together and no example underlines this better than the Jaguar whose whole reputation, indeed legend, was forged by its wins at the Sarthe circuit. Success in the smaller classes carried considerable weight as well as we see a broad spread of car manufacturers now anxious to throw their products before the public eye in the one race that mattered.

It was the Jaguar that was the star of the 1951 race. Their new C-type had been developed specifically to win this event and despite competition from nine Ferraris, six Talbots and Chrylser V-8 engined Cunninghams (the first serious American contenders for outright victory for twenty years) it achieved its aim and started that legend. Aston Martin again did well, Lancia made its first appearance with an Aurelia winning the 2-litre class, and a little known German make, having its debut too, was victorious in the 1100 c.c. class - its name: Porsche.

Next year Mercedes was ready to join in with their impressive 300SL model and the potential of this lured Jaguar into making a classic error - incorporating last-minute changes without fully testing the cars and the Coventry marque duly paid the price: all the C-types retired early on with overheating troubles. But the Germans did not have it all their own way, for a Talbot driven solo by Pierre Levegh was in the lead until the last hour when this remarkable drive came to an end with mechanical failure (induced by the driver's fatigue?), allowing the first German victory at Le Mans. Mercedes took the first two places with Hermann Lang (the pre-war Grand Prix driver and European champion) and Riess winning. Cunningham could only manage fourth behind a Nash-Healey but Lancia, Jowett, Porsche and Monopole all repeated their honours.

Jaguar quickly learned their lesson and the C-type was returned to 'normal' for the 1953 race except that, rather sensationally, disc brakes were fitted for the first time enabling much advantage to be gained by braking later into the corners. It was excellent timing on the part of Jaguar because this year saw the best entry by 'works' cars of any Le Mans race so far: no less than nineteen manufacturers' teams accounted for forty-eight entries, the only 'name' missing being Mercedes which had withdrawn from competition for a year to prepare their new Grand Prix onslaught. Here was the convincing evidence of the status of this classic race and it provided Jaguar (as did the disc brakes) with its most convincing win: all four entries finished led by Rolt and Hamilton. It also provided Cunningham with his best result over the years, a third place for the rigid-axle C-5R. Even Gordini finished sixth and Panhard won the Index with a car of their own construction.

Where were the Ferraris in these races? Alas, Maranello mechanical reliability was generally poor but revenge awaited them in the wet 1954 race which saw the debut of the D-type Jaguar. The big 4.9-litre Ferrari of Gonzales and Trintignant took the lead from the start but in the final stages nearly lost it to the Rolt-Hamilton D-type during a prolonged pit stop. Bristol won the 2-litre class while Porsche, steadily carving out an enviable reputation for speed and reliability, took both the 1.5-litre and 1100 c.c. classes. The presence of a privately-entered Triumph TR2 acted as a reminder that Le Mans was really intended for production cars - the sports-racers were by now really taking over, certainly as far as outright contenders were concerned.

And so we come to the tragic race of 1955, the year when the Mercedes of Levegh (invited to drive in recognition of his 1952 performance) was launched into the crowd of spectators opposite the pits at 6.35 on the Saturday evening. Over eighty perished, including Levegh, and the world of motor racing seemed to be doomed. The effect was predictably devastating: a temporary ban on motor racing in France, a permanent ban in Switzerland (effective even now), the end of masses of smaller races run in the provincial areas of the continent, thus eliminating a very colourful part of the motor racing scene, the cancellation of major Grands Prix such as the French and German . . To avoid panic the actual race carried on, the Hawthorn-Bueb Jaguar finally triumphing after Stuttgart had ordered withdrawal at midnight of the Mercedes cars (complete with air brakes to counter the discs) as a gesture of respect. Aston Martin had their best result to date when the Collins-Frère DB3S came second and Bristol, making their final appearance, took the 2-litre class once again. And Porsche? They came fourth, winning the 1.5-litre class and the Index as well.

It needed French national awareness of the race's importance and a club as strong and as wealthy as the A.C.O. to survive such a catastrophe but happily the Le Mans race did and a total rebuild of the pits area was the minimum required. The 1956 race was finally held at the end of July and is remembered particularly for Frère's embarrassing second lap spin in the Esses which eliminated two works Jaguars straight away! The third car having had engine problems, it was the splendid efforts of the Ecurie Ecosse D-type that saved the day for Jaguar. Aston-Martin again finished second and a Lotus X1 won its class, the first for the marque. D.B. Panhard won the Index for France once again and there was much relief that no major incident took place (although French driver Louis Héry succumbed to his injuries after crashing his open-bodied Panhard at White House). Le Mans certainly could not withstand another major blow and that remains true to this day.

Well-tried designs, we have seen before, generally form the right recipe for success in long-distance races and Jaguar reaped their harvest well and truly in 1957 when the D-types took five of the top six places, Ecurie Ecosse again obliging but this time with first and second. The opposition was not as powerful as it had been in 1953, the big

V8 Maseratis and V12 Ferraris soon falling by the wayside, but this was very much the D-type's hour, the British success being completed with Lotus' victory in the Index, much to France's chagrin!

A three-litre capacity limit was then set for the sports car championship and Le Mans dutifully fell into line. This did not suit the Jaguar engine but it did the Ferraris and Aston-Martins, the latter make's DBR1 cars now beginning to shine in sports car races. The 1958 race was rather reminiscent of that of 1954 - plenty of rain causing plenty of retirements and a win for a V12 Ferrari, this time in the hands of Phil Hill and Olivier Gendebien, a partnership destined to achieve further honours at Le Mans. It turned out to be very much Italy's year when the little 750 OSCA driven by de Tomaso (himself!) and Colin Davis (son of 1927 Bentley winner 'Sammy') snatched the Index category away from the French again. There were class wins for Porsche of course and a TR-engined Peerless GT, a true production car, also finished the race. The DBR1 Astons were too frail and a privately-run DB3S saved their face by taking . . . . . second place.

"Always the bridesmaid, never the bride" you could say was a summary of Aston Martin's fortunes at Le Mans. Having first run in 1928, the marque had taken part in every race since 1931 and now in 1959 their hour was finally to come. An innovation was to run two categories for Sports-Prototypes and Grand Touring cars, and there was an Index of Thermal Efficiency to support the Index of Performance. The idea was to bring more production-based cars to the line and it worked; there were even two-stroke Saab saloons in the 750GT class! Aston Martin's previous frailty became Ferrari's frailty and, as the red cars dropped out, the way was clear for the Feltham team to score a long-awaited one-two finish. A D.B. Panhard did at last retrieve the Index of Performance once more and its team-mate took the Efficiency prize as well, so the French did get some sums right! Surprisingly, Porsche won nothing that year, the only time in their history to date when none of their cars even finished!

Nevertheless, the Aston Martin success was a fitting end to a wonderful decade despite the horror of 1955 and if France had little to show for outright winners, it was the end of a splendid British era, for there were to be no more Le Mans-winning cars from this island for many years. It was also the last time a straight cylinder engine won the race. From the sixties onwards all victors were equipped with either opposing cylinder engines or even a rotary!

Ferrari on its way to the marque's first victory in 1949.
Frazer-Nash and Delage give chase.

Mulsanne Corner in 1951. Cunningham leads Jowett Jupiter, Ferrari and Nash-
Healey while D.B. and 4 C.V. Renault keep out of the way. The barren background
was the site of the military camp.

1953 - very standard Austin-Healey after leaving White House.

1957 Index of Performance winning Lotus XI 750c.c.

1955 - Dick Jacobs' MGA - shortly to crash - leads 'Bob-tail' Cooper in the Esses.

*1953 - winning Jaguar tears past OSCA on pit straight.
Notice the narrowness of the circuit!*

Aerodynamic Panhard heads 'standard' Triumph TR2 at Mulsanne in 1954.

Le Mans à la carte in 1959 – MGA, two-stroke SAABs, OSCA,
Stanguellinis and D.B. set off.

1962 - Brutal Maserati 151 is sandwiched by French-entered A.C. Ace
and class winning Morgan Plus Four.

*1964 – first appearance of Ford GT and last effort by Panhard flat-twin.
They pass crashed Triumph Spitfire.*

*1972 – Matra's first winning year. Second-placed Matra chases
Ferrari Daytona in the Esses.*

Chapter 6

1960 - 1965 Italian Superiority - Part 2

Throughout the history of the Le Mans race we can see distinct periods of domination by one particular marque: Bentley in the late twenties, Alfa Romeo in the early thirties and Jaguar in the fifties. The first half of the sixties belongs most definitely to Ferrari with its V12 in various guises. Indeed it was Ferrari that effectively propped up the top end of the race at that time since several hitherto key contenders, Mercedes and Jaguar among them, had in the meantime officially withdrawn from racing, the more to concentrate the minds of their engineers on production cars, and thus exploit the benefits of their hard-won prestige on the track.

A brief look at statistics underlines this domination by Ferrari. If we consider the first six positions in the six races from 1960-65, out of the total of thirty-six places, Ferrari secured no less than twenty-eight of them! In 1960 only the third-place private Aston Martin split a Ferrari clean sweep in the top six, in 1964 only the GT winning A.C. Cobra in fourth did the same, but in 1963 Ferrari had the top half-dozen places to itself, the Italian marque relying on a mix of sports-prototype and GT cars to achieve all this. No such total control of the race's honours had been exercised by any other make up to that point and the only repetition is to be seen in the early eighties by Porsche with the 956/962 series.

We have seen also how the sports-racing car, the issue of the A.C.O.'s tentative prototype category, had been gradually displacing the genuine production-based car and, in an attempt to restore some semblance of the original spirit of sports car racing, the new Appendix C regulations demanded 10-inch high windscreens and adequate luggage space. However the GT category (introduced to Le Mans in 1959) also helped to restore the balance and many production cars were still able to race at Le Mans during the sixties aiming at class wins.

In 1960 these new regulations encouraged twenty-five of the fifty-five starters to be fixed-head coupes and Le Mans welcomed back an American challenge in the form of Chevrolet Corvettes, three Briggs Cunningham cars and a Camoradi entry. This latter team also fielded three of the Maserati Type 61 'birdcage' sports-racers. Cunningham also had responsibility for running Jaguar's E-type prototype which was fast in practice but not yet durable. Nothing really constituted a serious threat to Ferrari although the early loss of two of their leading cars with empty fuel tanks caused alarm (Ferrari had increased the power since the April trials!). The winning Frère/Gendebien car had escaped a similar fate by coasting to its pit. Four of the delectable 250 GT Ferraris came home behind the third-placed private Aston Martin of Clark and Salvadori, the Tavano-Dumay car taking the GT category.

Porsche resumed normal service after its lapse in 1959 by winning the 1600 c.c. class and the two Lotus Elites not only took the 1300 c.c. class but also the Index of Thermal Efficiency. France was pleased to see D.B. Panhard retain the Index of Performance, and in true Le Mans tradition a sturdy MGA twin-cam with bored-out engine won the 2-litre category. This race was a notable triumph for Belgium: three of the first four drivers emanated from that little country.

The following year we can see an increasing trend towards the mid-engined concept. This was not new to Le Mans - Porsche had been consistently competing with cars with engines mounted ahead of the rear axle - but the success of the Cooper-Climax in the F1 World Championship of 1959-60 inevitably turned designers' minds to develop the theme more comprehensively. Ferrari dabbled with a 2.5-litre 6-cylinder mid-engined prototype alongside their V12 front-engined runners while Maserati produced three mid-engined Type 63s, two of which were run by Briggs Cunningham, still trying! For once there were no Jaguars (since 1950) but another privately-run Aston Martin DBR1 was accompanied by two Zagato DB4GTs. Another famous name returned with the appearance of two Sunbeams, one a Harrington Alpine which was, much to the team's surprise, to win the Index of Thermal Efficiency. Interest in the race was maintained by the efforts of the Rodriguez brothers in their NART Ferrari to defeat the 'works' cars but the latter came home in the first two places (the reliable partnership of Phil Hill and Olivier Gendebien scoring again) with one of the Maseratis managing an unexpected fourth. Once more the Index of Performance fell to a D.B. Panhard while the best Britain could manage was ninth with one of the prototype Triumph TRS cars although a Lotus Elite did win its class again.

For 1962 the sports car championship was replaced by a GT championship but the organisers of the main events decided to allow sports racing cars to run as before and the A.C.O. devised a class of 'Experimentale' cars with an upper limit of four litres. Ferrari and Maserati jumped at the chance, the latter with the Type 151 V8 coupés. Ferrari fabricated the 330LM; it was the last front-engined winner of Le Mans and there were no less than fifteen Ferraris in all at the start. Of special interest was the appearance of the GTO, the latest development of Ferrari's 250GT series, the prototype of which had run the year before in the hands of Baghetti and Tavano.

This race marked the return of Aston Martin, urged on by their French dealers. Their P212 ran with the leaders initially in the hands of Graham Hill and Richie Ginther but unfortunately did not last long. And Jaguar was back, albeit privately with the E-type, the Cunningham-entered car coming fourth followed by Peter Sargent's special coupé version. For the French, DB was no more, replaced on the one hand by Deutsch's production prototype CD Panhard coupés and on the other by René Bonnet's Renault-powered machines. Dispute over the power units was the cause of the split and when the Panhard-engined CD won the Index of Performance, it was round one to Charles Deutsch. The scrutineers rejected the Lotus 23s as 'not conforming to the spirit of the regulations'. A strange irony for the organisers had turned down the Morgan Plus Four for similar reasons the year before and now it was allowed in; it went on to win the 2-litre class!

The race was, not unexpectedly, a Ferrari-dominated affair (the Maseratis were as frail as ever) and interestingly the new GTOs finished second and third behind P. Hill and Gendebien's sports-racer. The FIA certainly had their way.

In 1963 the sports-racing prototypes were still there confirming the trend that has survived to the present day, but Ferrari was serious with the 250P mid-engined cars and one of these (Scarfiotti and Bandini) came to be the first machine of that configuration to win Le Mans. Aston Martin further developed their car into the 215 prototype and this was accompanied by some DB4GT versions and of particular significance was the appearance of Eric Broadley's new mid-engined Lola coupe which performed impressively: it was to be the basis of Ford's impending effort. A famous French name, Alpine, made its appearance at this race, although the team sadly suffered tragedy when Bino Heinz was killed. But the most unusual feature of the race was to be the whisper of the gas-turbine Rover-BRM which did not really fit into any category; Rover were still convinced of this power plants' future for road use and the car did indeed finish. Other finishers included an MGB, an A.C. Cobra and a René Bonnet which won the Thermal Efficiency Index, the Index of Performance going that year to the winning Ferrari.

The following year saw the start of mighty Ford's serious attempt to win. The American company was becoming increasingly competition-orientated and had even tried to buy up Ferrari in 1963 as a short cut to success. Those negotiations had foundered and now the two contenders were face to face. Three of the new GT40s challenged Maranello's usual array, the Italian marque's 250P having grown into a 275P thanks to a larger engine. And there was another attack from America, from Carroll Shelby's A.C. Cobra Daytona GT coupes. Ferrari had been hoping that his new 250LM would have been homologated as a GT despite his not completing the requisite one hundred examples but this piece of attempted rule-bending came to nought when Porsche, which had been quietly and regularly winning its class year after year, came up with the necessary number of new 904GTs. Two of the Ferraris raced as prototypes - their day was yet to come. Iso Rivolta made its Le Mans debut as did two (unreliable) Sunbeam Tigers. Down in the smaller classes, the rules now forbade engines of less than one litre: Charles Deutsch merely supercharged the Panhard twin and it competed (unsuccessfully) with the likes of Alpine, Austin-Healey Sprite, Triumph Spitfire (wearing the coupe bodies that presaged the GT6) and René Bonnet.It takes experience to get a sports-racer to win Le Mans and Ford had to learn the hard way. One car crashed and the others found that their gearboxes could not cope. This left Ferrari to dominate once more with the Vaccarella-Guichet 275P taking the win. A taste of future American power was however given to Maranello by the Gurney-Bondurant Cobra Daytona which finished fourth wining the GT class, the first time since its inception that Ferrari had not won this important category.

Ford of course was not to be deterred. In 1965 they arrived with even greater might: a six car team, two of which had huge 7-litre engines. Ferrari had a mass of prototypes, the factory concentrating on the P2 racers, but the presence of the now re-named 275LM was to prove fortuitous although it was still unhomologated. Unusually there were no contenders in the mid-field 2-3 litre class that year but seven Porsches led the smaller engined group with Alfa Romeo, MGB, Alpine-Renaults, Sprites and Spitfires lending support. The Rover-BRM returned, this time as a 2-litre and clothed in a smart coupé body.

Dearborn's brute force still lacked reliability but so did Ferrari's 'works' contenders and the Italians had to fall back on sheer weight of numbers, the NART 275LM of Gregory and rising star Jochen Rindt saving the day for Maranello. Their new GT car - the 275GTB - however took back its category, the Cobra entries only managing a poor eighth this time. The Rover-BRM led home the British contingent which claimed class wins for Sprite and Spitfire. And for the very first time in the race's long history, no French cars finished at all.

It was the end of an age - a remarkable run of six consecutive victories for the famous Italian marque - a total of nine in all. Perhaps equally impressive was the depth of Ferrari success - can we call this first half of the sixties Ferrari's golden era?

Chapter 7

1966 - 1969 Ford's turn

American might, so often decisive in world affairs, overwhelmed Le Mans in 1966 to an unprecedented degree. Ford was determined to be third time lucky and the American giant arrived in France with an armada of thirteen cars to combat all comers, especially Ferrari who were pitching three of the P3 (4-litre) models against the transatlantic invasion. Failure for Ford was unthinkable and the factory had eight 7-litre MkIIs (as seen in 1965) backed up by five GT40s. These, they hoped, would be decisive.

Unavailability of sufficient drivers for such a force presented a temporary problem, several key men such as Lloyd Ruby, A.J. Foyt and even Jackie Stewart being temporarily sidelined by recent crashes. But the omens were even worse for Ferrari when their best pilot, John Surtees, finally walked out, having reached the end of his tether with the absurd politics that had constantly bedevilled that team.

The regulations had once again been changed by the C.S.I., remoulding the character of Le Mans once more in the direction of outright racers. The popular GT class was now redefined to include cars of which five hundred had to be produced - thus only three entries, two Ferrari 275GTBs and a Porsche 911, came to the line. The prototypes, were left alone but a Sports Car Class was inserted, requiring fifty examples to be built and this was the category counting for the championship. Little heed seems to have been taken as 42 of the 55 starters came under the mantle of the prototypes.

Ford was somewhat optimistic after its successes in the early season Florida events at Daytona and Sebring and felt that the gearbox troubles which had dogged them previously were now cured. An unexpected threat to their prestige came from one of Jim Hall's Chaparral cars which only a month before had won at the Nurburgring, complete with a Chevrolet engine! Were General Motors to eclipse Ford at Le Mans after all?

Other new names that year included the first appearance of Matra cars, as yet just B.R.M. - powered, C.D. - Peugeot with transversely mounted 204 engines (the Panhard twin had finally gone!) and even a Mini-Marcos with BMC 'A' series 1300 engine. French interests were chiefly in the hands of Alpine-Renault whose period of real glory at Le Mans was about to unfold.

It did not take the Fords long to establish their domination of the race, the only interruption to their plans being the Rodriguez-Ginther Ferrari which nipped into the lead briefly on the Saturday evening. That apart the MkIIs stayed convincingly ahead while Ferrari began the downward curve that has denied the once supreme contender overall victory ever since - only two examples reached the flag in 1966. Ford tried to stage-manage a dead-heat but the difference in yards at the start meant that victory was awarded to the Bruce McLaren-Chris Amon car to the chagrin of Ken Miles who had led for most of the latter part of the race. For France, the little Alpine-Renaults swamped the Index of Thermal Efficiency with a 1-2-3 win and the Mini-Marcos finished, albeit in last place, the only British car to cross the line.

And so, despite many of their own runners falling out, America had finally triumphed at Le Mans after a hard road had been travelled, some forty-one years since a Chrysler had opened their challenge in 1925.

Ford had now tasted success and was hungry for more, this time hopefully with American drivers. Ferrari had in the meantime served notice that it was not giving up by finishing in the first three places at Daytona early in 1967, and the promise being shown by the new 'winged' Chaparral 2F meant that a truly titanic show-down was in store for the 24-Hour race. Ford had come up with the MkIV, still with seven-litres as the regulations once again permitted the large-engined prototypes to run. Four of these new models supported by three MkIIs and three GT40s contributed the Dearborn attack while Ferrari countered with seven P4 and P3/4 prototypes of four-litres. Aston Martin re-appeared in V8 engine form to power two Lola coupés and Lotus made an unexpected appearance with a Europa-based Type 47. Porsche arrived in increasing numbers at Le Mans at this period, having won the Index of Performance the previous two years and now poised to do it again. Matra was having another try in the midfield, albeit unreliably!

Battle royal was duly joined. Fords took the lead but Phil Hill's Chaparral challenged strongly and Ferraris were doing much better this time, the Parkes-Scarfiotti P4 working its way up among the leaders. When the Texan car succumbed to transmission failure, it was a straight Ford-Ferrari fight to the finish, despite three Fords being eliminated in a multiple crash in the Esses. Gurney and Foyt managed to stay ahead in their red MkIV keeping two Ferraris at bay and thus scored the first all-American win, achieved in true American fashion with all records broken and with the biggest engined winner ever at Le Mans. There was nothing more for Ford to prove!

Next year out went the big engines when the regulations limited prototypes to 3-litres, although cars of which over fifty examples had been constructed were permitted to run with their larger engines. And out nearly went the Le Mans race itself once again! 1968 was the year of serious student riots in France and we almost had a repeat of 1936 when the race was cancelled for political reasons. This time, thankfully, the day was saved but it was postponed and Le Mans had an unusual autumnal backcloth more reminiscent of the Paris 1,000 km races at Montlhéry as it slotted into the last weekend of September.

With the big litres gone, Ford's official contribution that year being the provision of a timely speed-reducing chicane before the pits, there was a change in the top cast: no works Ferraris, John Wyer entered GT40s, up and coming 3-litre Porsches and a new V-12 Matra accompanied by bigger 3-litre V8 Alpine-Renaults, these blue cars reflecting a genuine renaissance of French motor racing at that time. Alfa Romeo returned under the Autodelta banner but only with 2-litre V8s and there were two American Howmet turbine cars but their disappearance fairly early in the race signalled the end of attempts to pursue this form of motive power at Le Mans.

The flat-eight Porsches took full command in the early stages but gradually they failed and Pedro Rodriguez and Lucien Bianchi worked their way into the lead in typical John Wyer controlled fashion. Excitement for the home supporters and genuine signs of future success were provided by Pescarolo in the Matra which only lost second place when tyre failure caused too much damage just after mid-day on the Sunday. The big Alpines failed (save for one which finished a lowly eighth) but their smaller brethren clinched the Index of Performance for France after a six year interval. Once again only one British car finished, the little Austin-Healey Sprite bringing up the rear. How very different from the era of the fifties!

The 1969 race was to be memorable for several reasons. It witnessed the last Le Mans type start, the need to secure safety belts rendering the old tradition impractical. Porsche had circumnavigated the spirit of the ban on large engines by building twenty-five (the new homologation figure) flat 12 917s for the Sports Car Class and the race culminated in a breath-taking cut-throat Ford versus Porsche duel in the final hours that gave the GT40 a last victory by the smallest margin ever (excluding the fabricated 1966 dead-heat), some one hundred and twenty metres! Interestingly, the Porsche 917s ran the race using their moving rear wings (the last cars permitted to do so!) despite a sudden and total ban on such devices imposed by the CSI a few weeks earlier in Monaco following serious accidents in the Spanish Grand Prix.

The 1969 entry presaged the theme of sports car racing for the seventies: France versus Germany. Porsche had sixteen cars in all while Ferrari was down to four (including two works V-12s) - their smallest entry since 1954. Matra came armed with four V-12s and Alpine-Renault had four big and four little runners. John Wyer's GT40s were back hardly expecting any degree of success against the strong works contingents, yet Le Mans has always taught a lesson: controlled reliable speed invariably wins in the end.

The race began badly. John Woolfe, an amateur trying to master the devilish 917, lost control at White House on the first lap and lost his life. Porsches various, 908 and 917, led for most of the time while the Matras stayed in touch as did the Wyer Fords. However, when the leading German cars broke one by one, Ickx and Oliver (later of Arrows and Footwork fame) found themselves leading, by a short distance from Herrmann's sole surviving works Porsche. This set the scene for the famous 'Grand Prix' which was to bring Ickx the first of his record-breaking six wins at Le Mans. Matra had its first success in the race when three of their cars lasted the course and France won, with the little Alpine-Renault, the Index of Performance for the very last time.

Porsche had not yet won outright but all that was to change as Le Mans moved into the next decade.

Chapter 8

1970 - 1980 France v Germany

In 1870-71 France and Germany were at loggerheads in the Franco-Prussian War during which conflict there was, as mentioned, the Battle of Le Mans - the Germans won! A hundred years later the old protagonists were locked in battle again but this time in a more civilised and exciting struggle - to win the world's foremost endurance race.

As the seventies unfolded, we can trace the two main themes that influenced the historical path of the Le Mans race: first, the Porsches, after almost twenty years of continuous support, finally achieved outright victory, a pinnacle they would reach more often than any rivals; secondly, France was to experience the fruits of its motor-racing renaissance that had its roots in the mid-sixties. French cars were once again to take the major prize at Le Mans.

That first overdue victory for the famous German marque came at the start of the decade. The 1970 race turned out to be another 'big banger' contest, for Ferrari, unwilling to be outdone, had imitated Porsche's example and constructed twenty-five of their 512S five-litre machines so that they could run in the sports car category. No less than eleven of these lined up against a mere seven Porsche 917s, John Wyer now having the honour of managing the official cars. But Porsche made up for any imbalance at the top with sheer weight of numbers in the overall field: twenty-four of the fifty-one starters came from Zuffenhausen; any student of the race cannot fail to notice the consistently high number of Porsches that have made up the entries at Le Mans since the late sixties. The aerospace company Matra was continuing to hone its V-12 for future glory and more support for Italy came in the form of Alfa Romeo whose cars had grown up into full 3-litre versions. Of special interest now but hardly recognised as significant at the time was the first appearance of a Mazda rotary engine - albeit in a private Chevron chassis, but from small acorns ...... A Ligier replaced Alpine-Renault as France's contribution further down the entry list but it was not to be the mother country's turn quite yet. The real battle was between those big Porsches and Ferraris and in the very next race the verdict was decisive: Porsche not only scored its first outright win, with Hermann and Attwood at the wheel of a Salzburg entry, but the make triumphed in all the categories, even a VW-Porsche taking the GT class and seventh and last finisher.

The starting procedure for that 1970 event had been a compromise: the cars were lined up in their traditional echelon but the drivers were already strapped in. For 1971 a rolling start was instituted, behind a Porsche, which firm supplied thirty-three of the forty-nine starters that year! There were no Ferrari or Alfa teams to defend Italy but the famous Cosworth V8 made its race debut in a Ligier. The Index of Performance category, so frequently the source of salvaged French honour, was being run for the last time and it was won by the victorious Porsche 917 of Marko and van Lennep which set an amazing record of 3,315 miles covered at 138 m.p.h.

It was all change at the top in 1972 and out went the monsters again. A 3-litre limit for the sports class was slapped on, which certainly made sense for the Matra V-12! Something of the original character of 1923 was brought back by the creation of a TS category for Touring cars while GTS replaced GT, the Thermal Efficiency being valid for these two classes only. Thus we had Ford Capris versus a BMW2800CS, a welcome return of the German marque whose previous appearance had been in 1939.

The circuit had undergone some major surgery in the meantime, the notorious White House section now being completely bypassed by the new Porsche curves which in turn led to a more elaborate form of chicane just prior to the pit straight, all designed to slow the cars down in that high-risk area.

Expectation was high for a French victory, and the start being given by the French President himself, Georges Pompidou, served to reinforce the favourable omens. Opposition to the four Matras came from the Cosworth-powered Lola T280s and Alfa Romeos. Porsche relied on privateers, having been lumbered with redundant 917s! The Matras, to the joy of the crowd, made sure of overall success, two of them surviving to take the first two places and to register the first French win since Rosier's Talbot in 1950, with Pescarolo and Graham Hill in the victorious car. Sadly Jo Bonnier had lost his life on the Sunday morning when his Lola hit a Ferrari Daytona and flew off into the trees. But another Ferrari Daytona led home the GTS category and won the Index of Thermal Efficiency, while a Ford Capri V6 was the first Touring car.

1973 marked the fiftieth anniversary of the first 24-Hour race at Le Mans although it was in fact only the forty-first edition to be run. For such an historic event the entry did its best to live up to the occasion and the home-team of four Matras found itself confronted by a full works team of Ferraris, the last time Maranello made a serious attempt to win the race outright once more and thus add to its impressive tally of nine wins. The Italian team brought three 312 3-litre models and Wyer's two Mirage-Cosworth cars could not be discounted. Porsche came back under Martini colours with two Carrera RSRs, one of many 911 variations that we were to see over the years at Le Mans. Nor should we overlook the presence of the Sigma-Mazda, the first fully Japanese car to run in the race. The outcome was uncertain for most of the time and only the retirement of the Ickx-Redman Ferrari in the last hour left the Pescarolo-Larrousse Matra unthreatened and able to score a second French victory.

In contrast the field for the 1974 race was something of an anti-climax: no works Ferraris (Formula 1 was now their priority), no works Alfas and no works BMWs or Fords in the Touring category. The signs were certainly favourable to Matra once more, their chief opposition comprising the two Martini-entered turbocharged Porsche Carreras and Wyer's updated cars now called Gulfs instead of Mirages. In the event gearbox problems troubled the leading Matra and threatening Porsche but eventually the French team had its (and Pescarolo's) third straight win. With no more to prove the Matra factory finally gave up racing and the glorious shriek of that V-12 would be heard no more at the Sarthe circuit.

By the middle of the decade concerns had been mounting in motor-sporting circles about the amount of fuel being consumed in the wake of the oil crisis and the A.C.O. turned the 1975 event into an 'economy Le Mans', the regulations being tightened to permit no refuelling of the limited size tanks in the cars before the completion of twenty laps. This demanded a consumption of at least 7 m.p.g. and favoured especially the Cosworth V8. Wyer's Gulf-Fords, two Lolas and two of the three Ligiers were thus equipped. The Japanese were still trying, only this time the Mazda rotary was replaced by a Toyota turbocharged motor, and the reappearance of Alpine-Renault in the form of a 2-litre V6 prototype which was fastest in its class was to be of historical import. The presence of a BMW2002 saloon kept alive the links with the production cars of the past (it won its class), as did a Datsun 240Z. The Cosworth engines duly lasted - what a remarkable Grand Prix unit - and Wyer's cars sandwiched a Ligier (their best ever result in the race), Derek Bell accompanying Ickx in the winning car to forge a partnership which was to taste plenty more success in this great race.

We can draw a subsidiary line here for the A.C.O. provided the injection the race clearly needed by opening it up to a wider set of classes in 1976. The Group 6, 5 and 4 cars formed the main basis of the entry, a special invitation was extended to the Americans to bring their IMSA sports car and NASCAR stock cars, and a new GTP category was devised: this gave rise to the Rondeau cars (called Inaltera at first in deference to sponsorship) and the WM-Peugeot marque. Furthermore, the turbocharger, not new to Le Mans, assumed greater significance as several leading contenders were now so equipped: the 2-litre Alpine-Renault was in consequence upgraded to 2.8-litres and the Porsche-Martini works entries were led by their two turbo 936 spyders.

And so the Franco-German rivalry once more takes centre stage. The Alpine-Renault led at the start but soon had to give way to the Ickx-van Lennep 936 which proceeded to dominate the race, without threat after the French car had succumbed during the night. Alas, none of the American cars survived and a private Datsun killed its inexperienced driver, André Haller, a Strasbourg restauranteur.

43

Keen to pursue turbocharger development Alpine-Renault bounced back in 1977 with a major attack, bringing three works cars and a works-supported private entry, and the Renault turbo engines had now found their way into the Mirage team's two entries. Two Martini Porsche 936s were in the opposition camp backed up by 935s. The race was dramatic. Early problems left the leading Porsches in trouble: the Barth-Haywood 936 dropped right back, its fuel pump having to be changed, and Pescarolo over-revved his engine while challenging for the lead. This enable the French cars to monopolise the first three positions but a shrewd decision was taken to transfer Ickx to the Barth-Haywood car, quite in accordance with the regulations. Le Mans now witnessed a remarkable through the night recovery drive by the Belgian and, as the leading Alpines broke one by one under the pressure, Ickx was back in the lead! But more drama was to follow. With less than an hour to go this leading Porsche arrived at its pit billowing smoke and steam from a broken piston. There it stayed until the last ten minutes when Barth coaxed two final laps out of it to score an extraordinary win.

Renault could not give up now! And it so transpired that in 1978 four of the French contenders faced three Porsche 936s. The race mirrored that of the previous year in some respects: Porsche were in trouble early on, Ickx transferred to the most hopeful car, as an Alpine-Renault retired after twelve hours in the lead! But third time was to prove lucky for France. The Jaussaud-Pironi car, complete with bubble-top windscreen, had moved into the lead while the Porsche was having its gearbox rebuilt and managed to stay there until the end - Alpine-Renault had finally won at Le Mans and, as we have seen before, promptly withdrew from sportscar racing, the more to concentrate on F1.

And so for 1979 Porsche was almost left to its own devices, opposition coming from various Cosworth-powered runners, Lolas, Rondeaus, Mirages (now with Ford power once again) and two rather hopeless Japanese Dome-Zeros. The circuit had been altered slightly again with modifications at Tertre Rouge leading onto the Mulsanne Straight, and a 2 p.m. start was stipulated to encourage French spectators to partake in Sunday's elections. The Porsche 936s, the obvious favourites, unexpectedly broke, leaving a multitude of 935s to take charge - the German marque was being rewarded for the depth of its support over the years! Rain on the Sunday helped to nullify any speed advantage the remaining Group 6 racers had and the Ludwig-Whittington car finally triumphed, giving Porsche their fifth win. The outcome underlined once more a familiar Le Mans truth: endurance is more important than sheer speed!

In 1980 the A.C.O. tightened the regulations. Fuel delivery was slowed down and no mechanical component could be replaced once official practice had begun. A lack of works front runners meant that Rondeau's cars and a privately run Porsche 936 (but with Ickx at the wheel!) were expected to set the pace, the Porsche works efforts being confined rather strangely to a team of three 924 Carrera turbos! Lancia, now coming to the forefront of sports-car racing, was concentrating on Group 5 with its Beta Monte Carlo coupés in an endeavour to score Championship points, but these cars had little impact on the race. A Porsche 935 led initially, being overtaken by the Ickx 936 but this fell victim to its predictable weakness - the gearbox - and thus was Rondeau let into the lead in his own car, shared with Jaussaud. Rain late in the race caused some heart-stopping drama for the leader but the car survived and won, making Jean Rondeau the first man ever to drive a car of his own construction to victory in the Le Mans 24-Hours. To rub in the Gallic success, another Rondeau came third followed by a WM-Peugeot, the best result this little team was ever to achieve at Le Mans. It was to be France's twelfth victory (although the Rondeau used a British engine!) and we close the chapter with Germany and France scoring five wins each. All that was to change to a very one-sided contest during the eighties!

Chapter 9

1981 - 1987 Germany über alles
(The First German Period)

We can make two observations at this stage of the Le Mans story. First, this period witnessed the final disappearance from the entry lists of genuinely production based cars. The sports-racing car which first boosted the number of runners after the war finally took over, this development prompted as much by safety considerations about the even greater speed differential between the ordinary sports car and the out and out racer as by qualms about spectator appeal. Germany provided most of these last links with the original concept of Le Mans, although a single Ferrari 512BB did appear in 1984. Porsche had 924s running in 1982, unexpected 928S V-8s in 1983-84, and of course the ubiquitous 911 variants were reluctant to step down! It was the BMW M1 however which stayed the longest, an example running as recently as the 1986 race, but it was not classified at the finish. By the end of the decade Le Mans was reserved for specialised sports-racers, although some of these did make use of production-based engines such as the Jaguar V-12 and Mercedes V-8.

Secondly, just as the manifold and varied Ferrari entries formed the backbone of the race in the early sixties, so too did Porsche for most of the eighties, but with an overall supremacy quite unprecedented in the history of Le Mans.

This 'Porsche era' began with the 1981 race. A change of heart at the top of the company sent the twice victorious 936 back into action but this time wisely with a stronger gearbox, a former Can-Am four-speed design. It was worth it! Ickx and Bell led from the fourth hour and had a faultless run to bring the Belgian a record fifth win. Rondeaus were second and third, scooping the GTP category for the fifth time (although these cars had been labelled Inalteras at first) but it was not all joy for them for one of their number had crashed on the Mulsanne Straight claiming the life of Jean-Louis Lafosse. WM also encountered tragedy (a marshall being killed) when Thierry Boutsen had come to grief in similar circumstances just an hour after the 3pm start, a timing change from tradition once again to accommodate the needs of French voters. An assortment of Cosworth-engined machines, some with the new 3.3-litre DFL, had joined the Rondeaus in the chase of the Porsche: Lola, an ACR, De Cadenet, Ibec and Dome Zero. Further down the field we can note with interest the appearance of a GTP Porsche 924 Turbo using a still secret 2.5-litre engine (thus rendering it effectively the 944 prototype) and the Mazda 253s based on the RX7 and run by TWR. The four-cylinder Porsche survived to finish an excellent seventh but the Japanese rotaries did not last this time.

1982 opened a new chapter in sports-car racing with the advent of the Group C regulations, a formula which placed an emphasis on fuel consumption: tank capacity was limited and only twenty-five refuelling stops were permitted. As with all new formulae, there needed to be a period of transition and in this interim year cars of less than 2-litre in the old Group 6 category were still eligible. This let in two Lancia Martini turbo-charged contenders which were still able to compete successfully with the Group C newcomers.

This year saw the 50th running of the Le Mans race and it was marked by a worthy contingent of twenty-eight out of fifty-five entries which conformed to the new category. Prominent among these were the three new Rothmans-sponsored Porsche 956s, joined by two of Ford's C100s and Aston Martin representation once again in the form of the Nimrods, one from the works and the second a Pace Petroleum car. No less than sixteen of the Group C runners opted for the Cosworth motor, now available in 3.9-litre form as well.

The pattern of the race was one of steady elimination of Porsche's rivals: the Lancias dropped out early on, the works Nimrod crashed on the Mulsanne Straight, both Fords were gone by midnight and the vibration problems with the big Cosworth V-8 broke the Rondeau opposition by half-time. Porsche clearly stamped its intention of being King of Group C as its three new machines finished in line ahead with the potent and reliable Ickx/Bell partnership winning again.

A 'Junior' class was introduced in 1983 with a lesser fuel allocation and this provided a good hunting ground for Mazda - a rotary-engined 717 won the category and with Japanese pilots. Porsche strength was clearly manifested when, of the eleven 956s that ran, only two failed to finish, the marque taking nine of the top ten places, a BMW-engined Sauber being the only intruder in ninth position! Porsche was thus left to entertain the crowds and obligingly provided some drama towards the end: the Holbert/Haywood/Schuppan car was in the lead when the left hand-door flew off upsetting the flow of cooling air. This caused the engine to start seizing on the very last lap and only the sheer strength of the motor enabled it to stay ahead of team-mate Bells' rapidly catching car! Lancia had provided the most likely competition once more with its new Ferrari-engined LC2 Group C car but this was just not reliable.

Yet no works Porsche turned up for Le Mans in 1984! FISA had announced a further reduction in fuel allocation but rescinded this after both Porsche and Lancia had spent much money on the necessary engine development; the German's anger was expressed by withdrawal of the Rothmans-sponsored cars. There was, of course, no shortage of privateer support, however, and these successfully dealt with the Lancia opposition! The Joest car of Pescarolo/Ludwig took over when Wollek's Lancia dropped back after leading to give the French driver a fourth win. Aston-Martin effectively wiped themselves out of racing with a dreadful accident involving both cars on the Mulsanne Straight, a deflating tyre causing the shunt which seriously injured John Sheldon and killed a marshal. It was particularly unfortunate because Jaguar had come back to Le Mans in the guise of the American-inspired XJR5s from Bob Tullius' stable and it seemed like a renaissance of the fifties with the two famous British marques in battle once again. As it turned out, the Jaguars did not finish either, but it represented a fresh start which was, of course, to bear fruit later on. In the meantime Mazda's name was being clearly written in the Le Mans history books as their rotary engine once again triumphed in the secondary category, now known as C2, this time mounted in a Lola chassis.

This C2 class became increasingly popular and was well supported in 1985 with ten different marques struggling for honours. The reduced fuel allowance was finally implemented and ironically it seemed to affect the works Porsche 962Cs more than the marque's private customers. Thus we had something of a repeat of the previous year as the very same Joest car drove to victory again after a tussle with Richard Lloyd's Canon-sponsored machine. Lancias characteristically fell back. The IMSA Jaguars tried once more, only one of their cars reaching a poor thirteenth position with a broken piston but it was enough to let them win the GTP category! We note the first appearance of Toyota in this race and, significantly, Spice's success in his Tiga in C2.

In the interests of increased safety the highway authorities constructed a roundabout early in the following year at the Mulsanne corner with a slip road as a concession to the 24-Hour race. Competitors first experienced these modifications at the special test day in May. Among those present was the first four-wheel drive contender to run at Le Mans - the Porsche 961, which was to finish seventh in the actual race. 1986 is also remembered for the first appearance of the TWR Jaguars, three of which constituted a much more serious threat than their American forerunners. But Le Mans is not easily won from scratch and the XJR6s dropped out one by one, a burst tyre on the Mulsanne Straight - that ever present danger! - eliminating the team's final runner. The Sauber-Mercedes fell out early on as well but these two marques would have their turn in due course!

We were thus back to Porsches and the Bell/Stuck/Holbert works car fought it out with the now familiar Joest entry until tragedy struck at four o'clock on the Sunday morning: Jo Gartner's Kremer Porsche went haywire on the long straight, taking the young Austrian's life and putting the race under the temporary restriction of the pace car. The enforced slow running broke the engine of the private German car, leaving the works to triumph yet again. In the meantime the battle in C2 had been fought out among twelve different marques - such was the support, recalling the days of yore when there were plenty of contenders at Le Mans for the smaller classes - and victory finally went as a pleasant surprise to the Gebhardt JC843 entered privately in the best Le Mans tradition by the ADA Engineering team from West London.

The opposition to Porsche's supremacy was, however, steadily gathering momentum and in 1987 TWR mounted an even greater challenge with three XJR8 Jaguars. The Le Mans Test Day was held once again and once more we find a significant alteration made to the circuit: the fast curve after the pits - the Dunlop Curve, named in recognition of the famous footbridge - was replaced by a chicane at the behest of the motor cyclists who were concerned at the speeds attained at this point. New regulations required Group C cars to run on commercial grade fuel and this caused havoc early on in the race with the leading Porsches. Very soon only two strong German contenders were left running, the Bell/Stuck/Holbert car and that of Richard Lloyd which was to catch fire during the night. Was Jaguar being handed the race? Fate decreed otherwise for Win Percy was fortunate to escape from an enormous accident when a tyre burst on the Mulsanne Straight, Brundle's second-placed Jaguar retired on Sunday morning when a cylinder-head cracked, and Cheever's car could only finish fifth after gearbox and wheel bearing problems. The winner? Porsche of course, with yet another victory for Bell, Stuck and Holbert. A French Cougar, albeit with a Porsche engine as the constructor Yves Courage was the Porsche agent at Le Mans, finished third and Spice won C2.

History recorded that with this win Porsche's reign came to a close, but it had been a remarkable run of seven consecutive wins. No make of car had done that before and no other make had thus far scored twelve outright wins.

Chapter 10

1988 - 1991 "Redierunt, vicerunt"

In 1987 Jaguar won the World Sports Car Championship for the first time since the title's inception in 1953. The TWR team was serving notice that it was after the biggest prize of all: a sixth win for Jaguar at Le Mans. In January 1988 the Mercedes-Benz management gave more open backing to the Sauber-Mercedes team; they too were interested in genuine success. Porsche meanwhile was stepping backstage but even if the amazing 956/962 was no longer such a serious contender, albeit after an enormously successful innings, it was too early to discount it altogether, especially in twenty-four hour events. Porsche knew that and, leaving the championship series aside, was determined to make a special effort to win Le Mans yet again.

Prior to the 1988 race, the Mulsanne Straight was completely resurfaced and this urgent work resulted in the cancellation of the test weekend. Speeds had been growing alarmingly, with the first runners reaching 390 k.p.h. on each lap. In fact, during the race itself WM achieved its target of being the first Le Mans car to run at over 400 k.p.h. - it was timed at 405 k.p.h. (251 m.p.h.), an astonishing feat for a production-based engine.

The Mulsanne Straight was to have more say in the outcome of this race. The Sauber-Mercedes team soon found itself in serious tyre trouble, and, when during practice Klaus Niedwiedz suffered tyre failure at the notorious 'kink' towards the end of the straight, it was deemed discreet to withdraw the cars from the race; the Mercedes management had not forgotten 1955! This left the race open to Jaguar and Porsche, the British team bringing five XJR9LM cars to counter Porsche's three Shell-sponsored runners.

It turned out to be a fiercely fought contest. Porsche handicapped themselves early on when Ludwig tried to stretch out his fuel ration which forced him to drive half a lap very slowly in the car he was sharing with Bell and Stuck. It provided Jaguar with that extra advantage but let it be said that both teams had crucial failures in their fight to the finish. Engine trouble took out the Wollek-Schuppan-van de Merwe Porsche while its Andretti-driven team-mate lost performance with a piston failure. Transmission gremlins struck Jaguar, causing the loss of the car driven by World Champion Raul Boesel, Pescarolo and Watson and setting back the Sullivan-Jones-Cobb car which could only manage a lowly sixteenth place. More worrying was the engine failure of the Brundle-Nielsen Jaguar on the Sunday morning, but there was a welcome security in numbers this time for the Lammers-Dumfries-Wallace car stayed ahead long enough to bring Jaguar another win after thirty-one years. And, as anticipated, Porsches were competitive right to the end taking second and third places honourably with the Daly-Cogan-Perkins Jaguar fourth. From the outset Tom Walkinshaw had declared that he would need three years to win: one to accumulate race experience, two to bring a car to the finish and three to win! Interestingly, Ford needed the same in the mid-sixties. The British triumph was completed by Spice winning the C2 class, all very reminiscent of 1957, the year Jaguar and Lotus mopped up the major honours.

Jaguar had come back to win and Mercedes were to do the same but before we consider the 1989 race we must delve into politics. The governing body of motor sport, F.I.S.A., under the heavy-handed guidance of Jean-Marie Balestre, was seeking to package sport-car racing in much the same way as Formula 1, insisting on contenders running in all championship rounds, chiefly in deference, it was hoped, to the insane god television. Furthermore, the Group C fuel formula would be replaced by a 3.5-litre normally aspirated category, bringing sports car engines into line with those of Formula 1 and thus supposedly encouraging participation by manufacturers. This of course did not exactly fit the concept of sport-car racing, especially when it was envisaged that races were due to be reduced to short sprints. It certainly did not fit in with the whole concept of Le Mans, which was never conceived to cater for out and out racing engines of Grand Prix fashion, designed to last for limited periods only.

Le Mans was feeling threatened and, whereas the teams were given some leeway with current rules while they prepared for the new regulations, all was not well between the organisers, the A.C.O., and FISA. The row centred round the television and timings rights and a truce came only in May when the Le Mans race was dropped from the Championship. It was too late for competitors to change their minds and ironically Le Mans 1989 survived with a good entry.

Jaguar, having won the World Championship yet again, presented four cars. Sauber-Mercedes, now painted as Silver Arrows and with more than enough works backing, came back with three C9s. Aston-Martin also returned to the fray with two cars and Nissan had three of their new Lola-chassised machines, seeking that all important first Japanese win. Indeed we must not overlook the increasing Japanese participation, especially that of Mazda who had been quietly but surely learning the ropes - in 1988 they had brought their three cars to the finish and were to do so again in 1989. Porsches were by now reliant on private but generally capable teams, and WM was having a final fling after fourteen consecutive years of participation.

The race itself turned out to be a Mercedes benefit - their turn we might say. Jaguar, although well-prepared and quick, suffered all sorts of problems allegedly caused by vibrations induced by tyres turning on their rims. Endurance racing is like that and this year the British demise was rubbed in by the failure of the Spices to win in C2, this honour going to the Cougar-Porsche. There were a lot of cars catching fire at Le Mans in 1989 with fuel line failures causing some spectacular conflagrations among the Porsche and WM teams but there was equally major progress in fire and safety in motor racing and happily no harm came to any drivers. Mercedes, (in Sauber chassis) came home first, second and fifth providing them with only their second win (the first was in 1952 with the 300SL) since they first took part in 1930. Jaguar salvaged fourth and eighth and Aston-Martin only eleventh. Third ? Porsche of course, ever ready to step in should the more modern designs fail and, as we end the decade in Le Mans history, the Porsche 956 - 962 design must surely rank as one of the most outstanding designs ever to grace the famous Sarthe circuit.

As Le Mans entered the nineties, politics continued to dominate its very existence. Teams began to wonder seriously if the race had any future and while the television and timing rights battle simmered on, Balestre dropped his bombshell by declaring that any straight of two kilometres or more was banned forthwith! This seemed to sound the death knell of the race overnight but fortunately French government pressure (where else would this happen?) helped to dispel the threat not only to the race but also to the considerable tourist business annually generated in the whole Sarthe region. By February an agreement was hammered out: two chicanes were to be inserted along the Mulsanne Straight, a right-left just after the famous restaurant, and a left-right, 'Carte S', just before the kink. But Le Mans was not allowed to be part of the Championship and this factor discouraged Sauber-Mercedes from entering, feeling that they had nothing more to prove.

Jaguar, however, was definitely hungry for another win, Porsche was represented by a semi-works effort by the Joest team plus numerous privateers, and the big spenders in 1990 turned out to be Nissan who arrived with seven cars one of which took pole position by six seconds! A big 200 m.p.h. practice crash in which Jonathan Palmer eliminated one of the Joest Porsches served to remind everyone of the hazards of the notorious straight even with the need to slow down twice!

In the event Nissan made an early show of strength but their (Lola - chassised) cars had yet to prove durable and they gradually lost their front runners: Brancatelli knocked Suzuki's Toyota off at the Dunlop curve and when their last hope, the Brabham-Robinson-Daly car eventually succumbed, Jaguar was left in command with Brundle transferring to the Nielson-Cobb car after his own had broken, thus affording him a share in victory. Occasionally Le Mans holds back its dose of bad luck for the dying minutes and such misfortune visited the second-placed Brun Porsche whose engine let go with a mere fifteen minutes to run. Jaguar was the lucky recipient and the car that Konrad had damaged now took up station behind its team-mate - this made it seven wins for Jaguar! As two years previously, the British triumph was underlined by Spice once more making C2 its own.

Our story thus comes to the fifty-ninth edition and it really starts in July 1990 with the arrival of the demolition men. For a long time the dangers lurking in the narrow pit road had caused genuine anxiety, and the inadequacy of the whole pit complex was out of tune with modern racing facilities elsewhere. And so finally the structure which has symbolised the resurrection of the race in 1956, helping to wipe away the dreadful memories of the tragic accident of the year before came tumbling down to be replaced by an enormous and more spacious edifice offering the teams comparative luxury and the race administration the most modern facility possible.

The race itself was welcomed back into the Championship, for FISA had faced up somewhat to the reality that there were just not enough 3.5-litre cars available to form a viable field. They therefore craftily let in additional runners provided that the engine manufacturer was already participating in the Championship. This excluded Nissan and Toyota but let in the seemingly immortal Porsche 962 teams and Ford Cosworth-powered cars, whatever their chassis. Gone was Group C2 and instead there were two simple categories, number one for the 3.5-litre cars and number two for the others.

Teams such as Jaguar and Mercedes switched back to their more trusted and tried designs, casting their latest 'sprint' cars aside. The XJR12 and C11 had therefore unexpected new leases of life although fuel restrictions were intended to prevent them from running away as they wished. Peugeot, now contesting the championship in proper 3.5-litre form, made a welcome return to the race, the Sochaux marque having been represented down the years by WM, Constantin and Darl'mat since the company's own first and unsuccessful attempt in 1926, but their V-10 engines were known to lack the necessary staying power at this stage of their development.

The race made history for, once the leading Sauber-Mercedes had suffered overheating and the Jaguars were compelled to ease up to conserve fuel, the rotary Mazda took over and scored a sensational win, the first Japanese car to do so. How Nissan and Toyota must have wished that they too had entered the Championship! Yet it was a just reward because Mazda had consistently supported the race for years, steadily learning how to bring their cars home without fuss. And for the Japanese it was definitely the biggest prize of all, for Le Mans is unsurpassed in its prestige in the Land of the Rising Sun.

As the A.C.O. turned to the 60th running of its supreme race, we can take stock a little. So far two thousand eight hundred and fifty seven cars have started on the Saturday afternoon but we are as far removed now from those four-seater touring cars as it is possible to be, yet the glory available to a manufacturer is undimmed and unsurpassed. And it is likely that Le Mans would never have survived its tragedies, its trials and tribulations were it not French; only that nation understands sufficiently what it possesses in 'Les Vingt-Quatre Heures' to keep it alive even today. Vive Le Mans!

Porsche's first win in 1970

1977 Ickx's Porsche wags its tail at the Inaltera coming out of Tertre Rouge

1980 – first win for driver/constructor.
The Rondeau enters the chicane before the pits.

WM - Peugeot cuts in front of rotary-engined Mazda at the Porsche Curves in 1981

Four-wheel - drive Porsche
comes out of 'new' Mulsanne
corner in 1986 –
note the new roundabout.

McLaren wins first time out in 1995

Bugatti returns in 1994, with four wheel drive.

Privateers can still do well - 4th placed EMKA McLaren in 1998.

Chapter 11

GT revival as Second German Period begins

We have seen how the governing body was misguidedly trying to steer sports car racing into a package similar to that of the artificial and shallow world of Formula 1 by imposing a 3.5 litre atmospheric formula and reducing the endurance events to so-called 'sprints'.

But, of course, in their infinite failure to comprehend the real nature of sports car racing, the authorities were plunging this branch of the sport into one of its periodic doldrums. The Sports Car World Championship was about to wither away - major contenders such as Jaguar and Sauber-Mercedes had had enough, leaving only Peugeot with its new 905 and Toyota to fight for what was left.

This was the background against which the A.C.O. was contemplating its 60th 24-hour race and, not surprisingly, the number of entrants fell alarmingly. Had the club not squeezed an agreement out of the FIA to widen the scope of cars eligible, there would have been even fewer on the grid than the seventeen cars which lined up in 1930. As it was, only twenty-eight starters could be mustered to celebrate the anniversary in 1992.

The scheme involved admitting machines that met the old Group C regulations, as long as the entrant was participating in the world championship, or had a Porsche engine. How enormous is the debt of the post-war Le Mans to Porsche!

The front-runners in the 'atmospheric' camp were all V-10 powered, three Peugeots, three Toyota TS010s backed up by two Jaguar-based Mazdas with modified Judd engines, and two Lolas, Judd-powered as well. Against these in the 'turbo' camp were two Toyota C92Vs with 3.2 V-8 engines and three of the Le Mans constructed Cougars with the ubiquitous Porsche power. The rest were Porsche 962s, some Spices and even the BRM P351, the marque's sole participation as an entity. Some French national single-seater 'sports' cars were scraped in to bolster numbers!

The race fortunately did not fall apart and the V-10 engines proved surprisingly reliable over such a distance. In fact, fourteen cars finished, a 50 per cent rate, and Peugeot had its first win thanks to the efforts of Warwick, Dalmas and Blundell. This was the 13th French victory and the first for any engine of the V-10 configuration.

However, the A.C.O. was determined not to be caught out again. As the Sports Car championship fell into oblivion, the organising club announced in good time its intention to open its gates not only to the current Group C cars but also to those conforming to American rules and, most significantly to GT cars. Furthermore a new category of open car with a 425 b.h.p. maximum was encouraged.

1993 was something of a blank year in the history of sports car racing, but there was no shortage of optimism at Le Mans. The spring time test day was restored, and it was those GT cars which gave rise to promise. We had TWR with a team of Jaguar XJ220s, Lotus Esprits, a potent works Porsche 911 Turbo S LM and examples of the French GT marque Venturi. This all led to forty-seven starters while Peugeot pulled off a memorable 1-2-3 victory, recalling the similar French success of Lorraine-Dietrich in 1926. And Jaguar won the GT class, only to be disqualified on a technicality.

This GT renaissance was well under way by 1994 and if that year's winner, the Porsche-Dauer, was stretching the definition of 'road-car based' to its extremes, nevertheless the field for that year's 24-hour race included a host of genuine GT cars which were in themselves reminiscent of the real original intention of Charles Faroux and Georges Durand, the founders of the great event. Among the most exciting additions were Dodge Vipers, a Callaway Corvette, Ferrari F40, the return of a De Tomaso Pantera, Alpine Renault A610, a Porsche 968 Turbo, Honda with the NSX, a Harrier and even a Bugatti for the first time since 1939, this EB110S being only the third car to feature four-wheel drive in the history of the race.

All this variety and interest was the tonic the race needed in the absence of any FIA sponsored series, although the initiative of the BPR organisers saw to it that the new generation of GT cars had plenty of races throughout Europe to encourage development. 1995 therefore saw the club inundated with entrants: ninety-nine applications for forty-eight starting positions, this happy state of affairs forcing the A.C.O. to upgrade the spring test days into a full pre-qualification competition. This was the year when the McLaren F1 made its winning debut, a car conceived without competition in mind, but one of the few marques ever to win the great race on its first appearance. Lister and Marcos made welcome returns and the Ferrari 333SP made its first appearance, recalling the days when Ferrari open prototypes were for a time the staple diet of Le Mans just as Porsche were to become. And Honda had its first success at the Sarthe circuit by winning the GT2 category.

In fact, we find the mould of endurance racing by this time splitting cleanly into the two categories of open prototypes and GTs but a spanner came into the works in the 1996 race with the appearance of the Porsche 911 GT1. A beautiful car certainly but it was the start of turning the road-based GT cars into closed prototypes, underlined by its competitive second place to its TWR prototype winning stable-mate of Reuter, Jones and Wurz.

This upgrading of the GT1 category spilled over into the 1997 event. Three Nissan R390s challenged the Porsches aided by upgraded McLaren GTRs and the new American challenger Panoz, a name to count increasingly in the word of sports car racing. Its front/mid-engined layout echoed the Lister and Marcos contenders.

The intensely-fought pre-qualifications claimed sadly a life when the promising young French driver Sebastian Enjolras became victim of a horrendous fiery crash in his W.R., yet the recent history of Le Mans has been characterised by so little injury to the drivers, a satisfying achievement given the huge diversity of ability and experience inevitably brought together when running a long-distance race with some forty-odd starters.

Fire played its part (happily without injury) during the race, one McLaren non-starting while another made a spectacular show on the Mulsanne Straight in the final hours.And fire in the leading Kelleners Porsche GT1 handed victory once again to the Joest team TWR prototype, this time Alboreto, Johansson and Kristensen carving their names in the history books.

By 1998 the GT1 category was really getting out of hand. The FIA had ominously taken over the flourishing BPR GT series and with the advent of the extraordinarily successful Mercedes in the series, interest among manufacturers dropped off - these so-called GT cars were now outright racers. Yet the sheer prestige of success at Le Mans attracted firms such as Toyota, Nissan and BMW to concentrate almost solely on this event. That rarely ever produces the longed-for victory, as race experience is an essential ingredient and prelude to finishing let alone winning the 24-hour race. It did not stop these teams from trying, and Toyota came up with its GT-One to take on Mercedes with the CLK-LM, Nissan's now reliable R391, BMW's new V-12 prototype and Porsche's final rendering of the 911 GT1 in 1998 guise. The latter, with all that company's experience, won through in the end, despite being beaten in the world series totally by Mercedes. The Stuttgart cars, however, went home very red-faced from the big event that mattered, both cars retiring within the first two hours. The GT2 category beneath all this factory activity was now starting to go to the well-run Chrysler Vipers, true GT cars. And a privately-run McLaren, that of O'Rourke, Sugden and Auberlen, achieved a superb fourth place among such exotic company in the best traditions of Le Mans and forty years after a private Aston DB3S came second.

The 1999 race reflected the enormous rivalry between major manufacturers to win prestige in the market-place. Nissan tried once more, this time with an open-bodied prototype (one demolished itself in practice) and Toyota threw every ounce of effort into their attempt to win, albeit without that vital preliminary race programme. This necessity certainly paid off for newcomers Audi and even more so for BMW, whose revised car came out on top, beating Toyota into second place. Once again a jinx haunted Mercedes whose well-tested but as yet unraced CLR model caused enormous alarm. Two times their cars literally took off into the air with an obvious aerodynamic flaw during the practice sessions yet their management failed to react prudently as they had in 1988 when serious tyre problems afflicted the Sauber-Mercedes cars in practice causing their immediate withdrawal. Sheer good fortune came to Stuttgart's rescue when Dumbreck's Mercedes flipped over the trees into an empty trackside area on the Saturday evening of the race. That was it for the company - they at last pulled out, and these cars were never to race again.

BMW's victory for Winkelhock, Martini and Dalmas, the latter's fourth win, putting him on a par with Gendebien and Pescarolo, was fittingly scored with a V-12 motor, exactly fifty years after Ferrari had first done the same. And for BMW it was a first win, just as it had been for Ferrari as well.

The latter part of the decade was marked by two significant developments. First, the A.C.O. agreed to lend its name and support to a series of sports car races held in America by Don Panoz who was attempting to put some order back into the confused regulations that were prevalent on that northern continent. This American Le Mans series was open to cars conforming to the A.C.O.'s formula and was inaugurated in October 1998 by an event aptly titled the 'Petit Le Mans' run at Atlanta. The French club has always welcomed warmly any links with America and this move was intended to guarantee a plentiful supply of entries amidst the continued muddle created by the F.I.A.

Secondly, a new category, rather unhelpfully labelled GTS, was added to the 1999 regulations. Initially poorly supported, in nevertheless was an equivalent of the GT3 category which had steadily gained favour in Europe and which caters for genuinely road-based GT cars with little permitted modification. It leads us back to the real intention behind the GT car once again and takes Le Mans back to its roots while the prototypes provided the spectacle the public clearly wants alongside.

Chapter 12

"Toujours les Allemands"

The final year of the century and the dawn of a new millennium found sports car racing in a more healthy state than a decade previously. The American Le Mans series had been growing in strength despite a European sister series not surviving increasingly weak support. John Mangoletsi's sports-racing series (initially ISRS) had earned in 2001 FIA approval and championship status (Sports Car Championship), the races providing a competitive platform on which marques such as Dome and Ascari could score their first wins. And the American Grand-Am series catered for the private teams, encouraging the emergence of some sound contenders which found their way into the entry lists for Le Mans.

With so many sports/GT cars around, it was not surprising that many of them aspired to success at Le Mans. The organisers thus found themselves in the fortunate if difficult position of being well over-subscribed with entries, the result being that some very professionally competent teams were unhappily rejected each year. And at this stage the A.C.O. took the opportunity to re-define the classes of cars eligible. The prototypes fell into three groups: open cars ran in either LMP900 (minimum weight 900 kgs) or LMP675 (minimum weight 675 kgs) while closed prototypes were classified as LMGTP (minimum weight also 900 kgs). Modified GT cars (minimum weight 1100 kgs) became LMGTS while those with only minor changes ran in the LMGT category (again with 1100 kgs minimum weight).

The Le Mans races at the turn of the century were dominated by Audi, the Ingolstadt company wisely delegating the running of the racing team to that seasoned expert Reinhold Joest. As we have seen, he already had four Le Mans wins to his credit (Porsche 1984-85, TWR Porsche 1996-97) and had been a successful sports car driver prior to that.

He first raced at Le Mans in 1969 coming sixth in a private Ford GT40, his best result being 2nd in 1980 with Jacky Ickx in a works-lent Porsche. Audi was not a name normally associated with sports car racing, indeed their only involvement with Le Mans had been the DKW engine which Charles Deutsch chose to power his Index of Performance contender in 1963. But all that was to change. With characteristic Teutonic thoroughness, the ground was prepared by putting two of their touring car drivers, Pirro and Capello, into a McLaren to gain Le Mans experience in 1998. Then two open roadsters and two coupés came to the line in 1999, the former finishing impressively in third and fourth positions, the latter failing mechanically, chiefly because of late development.

The withdrawal of the likes of BMW, Nissan, Toyota and Porsche left the stage clear for Audi in 2000 and their R8 became the car to beat in sports car racing generally, the Joest magic quickly putting the cars in a league of their own - for example gearbox and rear axle units could be changed in the pits in just five minutes!

Pitted against these was a resurgence of interest from America; Cadillac, intent on reviving its image in world markets, elected to launch a programme aimed at winning Le Mans. Two private Cadillacs had run in the 1950 race as the first stage of Briggs Cunningham's admirable campaign to score America's first victory and now four prototypes (two delegated to the French DAMS team) came to do battle. But they underestimated the challenge before them and their Riley and Scott constructed chassis disappointed, a lowly nineteenth their best showing. Chrysler, in 1925 the first American manufacturer to be represented in the race, opted for a toe-in-the-water return. Their Mopar V-8 was installed in two of the new Reynard 2KQ chassis, these being entrusted to Hughes de Chaunac's ORECA team, which was about to score a hat-trick with its well-tried Vipers in the GTS category. But the Reynard chassis was fundamentally flawed and Nigel Stroud (the designer of Mazda's 1991 winner) was hastily co-opted to add some much-needed rigidity; the failure of the 2KQ in sports car racing was a contributory factor in the marque's sad demise a year or so later. With the Vipers showing Chevrolet's C 5-R Corvettes the way home, the ORECA Reynards could only manage a twentieth place at the finish, its team mate having retired on the first lap! It was left to the open Panoz roadsters to salvage American pride in the big prototype class.

But the honour of best after the Audi 1-2-3 clean sweep came from an unexpected quarter: the new team run by Henri Pescarolo, the four-times winner, gave France back some of its long lost glory by bringing home in fourth overall its Courage C52 powered by a V-6 turbocharged Peugeot engine based on that found in the Sochaux manufacturer's recently released top of the range 607 model. The preparation had been entrusted to the Sodemo firm from Magny-Cours. Further large manufacturer interest, if unofficial, was the first appearance of Volkswagen mechanicals at Le Mans. The French ROC team installed turbocharged units in two adapted Reynard 2KQ chassis, the resultant machines being fast but still too frail to win the P675 class. This went finally to the Lola-Nissan, a WR the only other class survivor.

And so as Germany continued to take the top honours, Le Mans moved from the twentieth into the twenty-first century and when Audi expressed its hunger for more, it was clear that business would be as usual. And thus it turned out because their two entries for the 2001 race did their duty, the same crew of Biela, Pirro and Kristensen handling the wet race best of all. Rain certainly played a crucial role that year, bright sunny periods being frequently interrupted by exceptionally violent rain storms which accounted for several contenders in the opening laps alone, the Pilbeam's first appearance cut short thus.

The race was also characterised by the return of two famous English marques: Bentley and M.G. The former, the mother company by this time part of the Volkswagen Group, featured an Audi engine in an LMGTP coupé, and one of the two entries finished fittingly third behind its cousins! The two M.G.s were Lola-designed P675 contenders with new AER turbocharged fours and the inclement weather gave them a welcome chance to show their potential before the inevitable mechanical problems caught up with a previously unraced design. This smaller prototype class was won by one of the previous year's Reynard-Volkswagens which coped with the difficult conditions very well to finish an astonishing fifth overall, reminding us that success at Le Mans does not necessarily go to the latest design, Ecurie Ecosse's success in 1956 with the well-tried D-type Jaguar being one such precedent.

And what of the continuing American campaign? Chrysler had let ORECA commission a Dallara chassis and a creditable fourth place was their reward while the Chevrolet Corvettes had the GTS class trophy to take home, beating the new potent Saleen S7R where it mattered! Alas, Cadillac could do no better than fifteenth.

The lure of a hat-trick was too much for Audi who headed the 2002 entry list (the 70th race) with three cars this time to allow for possible mishaps. Acceptance that no other car could seriously threaten their reign meant that interest centred chiefly around who was going to be the "best of the rest". Bentley returned with just one entry but with a bigger 4-litre motor, ORECA had substituted the V-10 Judd in the Dallara chassis as Chrysler withdrew all official support, and Nigel Stroud had cast his experienced wand over Cadillac which henceforth had a more state-of-the-art chassis even if it was still off the pace.

The M.G.s were back and were very fast, the two 'works' cars being supported by an American private entry and the English revival theme was continued by the reappearance of a Morgan, forty years after the traditional Malvern manufacturer had scooped the 2-litre class in 1962. And Le Mans had the first Dutch car ever to run in its history - the Spyker C8 Double 12-R, reviving one of the motor industry's oldest names and the one which first offered the public a four-wheel-drive car.

The Prancing Horse of Ferrari was seen again, three private Modenas and Prodrive's very quick 550 Maranello, but the famous firm was long out of Le Mans trim and all failed to finish, the bigger one catching fire in the Porsche Curves. Fire consumed the American M.G. on the Mulsanne Straight during the night as well while its team-mates sadly broke down once again. The Morgan Aero 8 GT(N) lasted much longer than expected, its engine giving up on the Sunday morning, but the British flag was kept flying because the Bentley once more was the best of the rest.

On paper the results uncannily mirrored those of the previous year, even to the extent that the winning drivers were identical; they were, in fact, entering the record books by scoring the first hat-trick of the same winning crew. ORECA brought its Dallaras behind the Bentley, which was the GTP winner again, and Chevrolet and Porsche won the GTS and GT category. Even the P675 class went to a Reynard-Volkswagen once more but only in the last five minutes when the WR had a rear suspension failure and watched its class lead evaporate as it struggled across the finishing line with one front wheel in the air!

Nothing is final at Le Mans until the car has actually crossed the line!

Landmarks and Headlines

1923 33 starters, all French except two Belgian Excelsiors and one private Bentley. Only time race runs in May. Two Rolland-Pillains with closed bodywork, two air-cooled S.A.R.A.s. Win for France (3-litre Chenard et Walcker) and only three cars fail – one S.A.R.A. has the doubtful honour of being the first retirement in Le Mans history. A 2-litre Bignan comes third and wins that class.

1924 Race in June henceforth. Winning Bentley challenged by Lorraine-Dietrich (2nd/3rd), 4-litre 8 cylinder Chenard et Walcker burnt out. Cars had to do twenty laps with hoods erected after completing five laps. Chenard et Walcker wins 2-litre class.

1925 American Chrysler and Italian O.M.s and Diattos add international character to race. Hoods had to be up at the start which was located just this once on Mulsanne Straight. First Le Mans-type start. 3-litre Sunbeam comes 2nd to Lorraine -Dietrich as two Bentleys retire as does an Austin Seven! Chenard et Walcker "tanks" win not only the 1100 c.c. class but also the Biennial and Triennial Cups. Unexplained accident claims life of Marius Mestivier (Amilcar) on Mulsanne Straight - first fatality during the race. Two Italian O.M.s cover exactly the same distance and share 2-litre class!

1926 Index of Performance (handicap division) added - O.M. the first winner. Lorraine-Dietrichs take first three places, as three Bentleys fail. First appearance of Peugeots (two sleeve-valve 174s models which retire). French E.H.P. wins 1500 class.

1927 First front-wheel-drive participant (Tracta). Big White House crash. Surviving damaged Bentley wins after French 3-litre Aries fails, having led for 17 hours. Winning margin (350 kilometres) the biggest in the race's history. 1100 c.c. Salmsons 2nd and 3rd! French S.C.A.P. the first 1500 to finish.

1928 Abandonment of need to use hoods. A.C.O. officially recognises general classification. Bentley defeats American Stutz. Chrysler '72's finish 3rd and 4th. Front-drive Alvis wins 1500 class and an Itala the 2-litre class.

1929 Pontlieue hairpin foreshortened. First 2-stroke to run (Tracta-Cozette). Bentley takes first four places. Winning car is Speed Six 'Old no.1'. Lea-Francis wins 1500 class and a Tracta the 1100 category.

1930 Smallest entry - 17 cars. Women crew for first time (Mareuse/Siko-Bugatti). Single Mercedes (Carraciola/Werner) fights Bentley team plus supercharged versions. Woolf Barnato (Bentley) scores his third successive win once again using 'Old no. 1'. Last Bentley victory. British Talbots 3rd and 4th. Lea-Francis again victorious in the 1500 category, Tracta again in the 1100 c.c. class. Private Alfa-Romeo is the marque's first appearance.

1931 Dramatic failure of big 5-litre Bugattis. Alfa-Romeo (Birkin-Howe) brings Italy's first success and the first for a supercharged car. Only 6 finishers. Private Mercedes SSK takes 2nd place. Private Lorraine comes 4th and Aston-Martin scores first success in 1500 class. First appearance by M.G. (two Midgets - both retire).

1932 Pontlieue section superceded by new "Esses" link to Tertre Rouge. Raymond Sommer drove 21 hours (Chinetti unwell) to victory in his private Alfa-Romeo. British Talbot again 3rd, Aston Martin again victorious in 1500 class. Amilcar takes 1100 c.c. category.

1933 Nuvolari (his only participation) wins by ten seconds after the lead kept changing in the final hours. Mme Siko escapes from overturned burnt-out Alfa Romeo. M.G. C-type wins 750 class. Riley 4th behind Alfa-Romeo and 1100 c.c. class winner. Another class win for Aston Martin.

1934 Last of Alfa-Romeo's four victories with the 8C 2300. Riley 2nd and 3rd.

1935 Entry predominantly British. Red Lagonda fends off private Alfa-Romeo.

1936 Race cancelled.

1937 Strong French contenders reflecting team's emphasis on sports car racing. Serious crash at White House early in race costing the lives of Pat Fairfield (BMW) and René Kippeurt (Bugatti). First French win (Bugatti) since 1926.

1938 More that half the starters are French. First appearance of a V-12 motor (Delahaye). French take first five places with 6-cylinder Delahaye the first winner with independent front suspension.

939 Climax of French domination as Bugatti leads home Delage. Simca Cinq (566 c.c.) the smallest engine ever to run in the race, and wins the 750 c.c. class.

949 "Prototypes" admitted to boost entry. 4 c.v. Renault is first rear-engined participant, the Delettrez the first diesel, Gordini TMM is the first to have a central driving position. Ferrari's victory is the marque's first of nine and first for a V-12 motor.

950 First of ten successes in the Index of Performance for the flat-twin Panhard motor (Monopole, D.B., Panhard). MAP diesel is the first to take part with a centrally-mounted engine. Jowett Jupiter is the first to win an award with a horizontally-opposed (flat) engine (1500c.c. class). Last French victory (Talbot) for 22 years.

951 Jaguar's first success (C-type). Porsche makes its first appearance in the race (356) and wins 1100 c.c. class.

952 Pierre "Levegh's" extraordinary single-handed drive in Talbot fails in final hours and hands victory to Mercedes-Benz (300SL), Germany's first win and the first for a car with closed bodywork.

953 Largest "works" participation - 48 out of 60 starters. Jaguar wins with disc brakes. Tom Cole (Ferrari) killed at White House.

954 Big 4.9-litre Ferrari nearly loses the wet race to the new D-type Jaguar.

955 World's worst motor racing disaster: 82 spectators killed when Levegh's Mercedes leaps into the crowd, claiming his life as well. Mercedes team withdrawn when leading, leaving victory to Jaguar. MGA prototypes run, two finish, one crashes (White House). Factory team of Triumph TR2s finish, Porsche 550s win 1500 class, Bristols again the 2-litres. Non-finishers include Lotus and V-12 Lagonda. Strange 'twin-boom' Nardi blown off course.

956 Race postponed to July to accommodate total rebuilding of the pit/spectator enclosure area. Ecurie Ecosse saves Jaguar's honour after two thirds of the "works" team eliminated on the second lap. French Talbots now Maserati engined retire. Lotus wins 1100 c.c. class. Louis Héry, garage-owner from Nantes, succumbs to injuries after crashing his Panhard.

1957 British triumph as Jaguar fills the first four places and Lotus (750 c.c.XI) wins the Index of Performance. Belgian Ferrari wins 2-litre class and Lotus again the 1100 category. Big V-8 Maseratis contest the lead but fail. Last appearance of Gordini and Talbot which fails to start.

1958 Prototypes limited to 3-litres to conform to new World Sports Car Championship rules. Very wet race with rain for 15 hours and 15 accidents, one resulting in death of Jean-Marie Brousselet (French-entered Jaguar D-type). OSCA wins 750 c.c. class. A Peerless finishes 16th.

1959 April Test days introduced. Index of Thermal Efficiency introduced. Entry divided into "prototypes" and GT classes. Only win for Aston Martin and only 13 of the 53 starters finished (28 per cent). No Porsches finished! 2-litre class goes to an A.C.-British and a Lotus Elite takes the 1500 c.c. class. Two 2-stroke Saabs take part, one finishing 12th! GT Ferrari comes 3rd, establishing a trend.

1960 New C.S.I. regulations stipulated 10 inch depth windscreens and requirements for luggage space. Ferrari wins against private opposition. First appearance of Chevrolet Corvettes. M.G. Twin-cam wins 2-litre class. Team of three experimental Triumphs finish but one unclassified. Maserati "Birdcage" competitive at start. Début of Lola marque. Austin-Healey Sprite wins 1000 c.c. class.

1961 Eleven Ferraris started bringing further success to Maranello with absence of serious "works" opposition. Sunbeam Alpine wins Thermal Efficiency Index. Maserati Type 63 finishes 4th, the marque's last result. First mid-engined D.B. finishes 19th. Triumph team finishes intact.

1962 Ferrari's win is last for a front-engined car, C.D. Panhard's the last Index win for the flat-twin Panhard motor. Lotus 23 excluded from starting. Aston-Martin returns with single entry (P212). Morgan wins 2-litre class and René Bonnet the 1000 c.c. class. Jaguar E-types come 4th and 5th. Both TVR and Marcos retire, as does the Ecurie Ecosse Tojeiro-Climax, Britain's first enclosed mid-engined sports-racer.

1963 Rover-BRM the first gas-turbine car to participate. First 100% Italian win (Scarfiotti/Bandini-Ferrari) was also the first victory in the race for a mid-engined car. Thermal Efficiency Index goes to René-Bonnet. Alpine marque makes its first appearance but fiery crash costs life of Bino Heins. Lola GT (forerunner of Ford GT40) crashes. Lotus Elite wins 1300 c.c. class.

964 Minimum engine capacity of 1000 c.c. introduced. Ferrari finish 1-2-3 but A.C. Cobra wins GT category. Alpine's first success with class win and Index of Thermal Efficiency. First appearance of an ISO Rivolta which wins its class. Two of three Triumph Spitfires crash. Alfa-Romeo TZ wins the 1600 c.c. class. Début of Ford GT40s, all three retiring. Last appearance of Panhard flat-twin motor, in CD Panhards (supercharged) - both retired. Sunbeam Tigers fail to finish.

965 Strong Ford entry (including two 7-litre MK 2s). "Works" cars fail in Ford-Ferrari battle, leaving private Ferrari (275 LM) to give the Italian marque its ninth and final victory.

966 13 Fords faced 10 prototype Ferraris, with the Detroit firm taking the first three places with the closest ever finish - 20 metres! This was the first time America won Le Mans and the first time a V-8 engine succeeded.

967 Last Ford-Ferrari battle, won by Ford MK IV (Gurney/Foyt), a 100% American win. Chaparral introduces high wing and automatic transmission. Factory Ferraris (P4) come 2nd and 3rd.

968 Political unrest postpones race until September. Artificial chicane, the Virage Ford, introduced at the approach to pits. C.S.I. limits prototypes to 3,000 c.c. thus excluding the big Fords and "works" Ferraris. John Wyer's Gulf team Ford GT40 (sports class) wins after excellent performance by Pescarolo in Matra. Howmet turbine cars fail. Return of "works" Alfa-Romeo (T33) which win 2-litre class.

969 Last use of the Le Mans-type start. Jacky Ickx (Gulf Ford, using same chassis 1075 as in 1968) wins by 120 metres from Herrmann's Porsche. First appearance of big Porsche 917. Serious accident at White House on first lap. John Woolf killed in his private Porsche 917, which also eliminates one "works" Ferrari. First finishes for Matra.

970 Wet race brings first Porsche win (917 Attwood/Herrmann), the Stuttgart marque winning all the categories! First victory for a "flat" engine. First participation by a rotary-engine (Chevron-Mazda). Unusual starting arrangement: drivers strapped in cars which were lined up in echelon. Eleven big Ferrari 512s cars challenged Porsche, seven succumbing to accidents, two finishing 4th and 5th. All Alfa-Romeos (3-litre) fail. Porsche 914 wins 2-litre class. Only 7 finishers, with nine unclassifieds.

1971 33 out of 49 starters were Porsches. First use of a rolling start. Porsche 917 (Marko/van Lennep) covered the greatest distance (3,315.203 miles) at the fastest average of 138.133 m.p.h., winning the Index of Performance, the last time this category was awarded. Début of Ligier.

1972 White House section of road by-passed by new Porsche curves incorporating new approach to the pit area. C.S.I. outlawed the big Porsche and Ferraris. First Matra success (Pescarolo/Hill), Graham Hill thus the first ever to win the Formula 1 World Championship, the Indianapolis 500 and Le Mans. Touring cars re-admitted to the race. Ford Capri beats BMW to Touring prize. Alfa-Romeo finishes 4th. Fatal accident to Jo Bonnier (Lola) on Sunday morning.

1973 Matra defeats Ferrari (312 P/B). First appearance of a Japanese contender (Sigma-Mazda). BMW wins Touring class. Both Gulf Mirage-Fords retire. Ferrari Daytona repeats previous year's success.

1974 Third win for Matra (and Pescarolo) against weaker opposition. Ferrari Daytona again triumphant in its category. Porsche turbo RSR second.

1975 A.C.O. introduced a fuel-consumption formula in response to the fuel crisis. Race therefore lost world championship status. First win for the obiquitous Cosworth V-8 in Wyer's Gulf-Mirage (Ickx/Bell). Strong competition from Ligier (JS2), one of which comes 2nd. Datsun 240Z wins its class, first Japanese success. Sigma used turbo Toyota engine but retires. First appearance of a Mazda.

1976 Wider regulations admitted IMSA and NASCAR entrants. No Ferrari took the start. Porsche's victory (Ickx/van Lennep) was first for a turbocharged car. De Cadenet's private Lola (T380) finishes 3rd. First appearance of Inaltera (Rondeau) marque. Alpine Renault Turbo A442 puts up fastest lap. Début of WM. NASCAR contenders (Ford Torino and Dodge Charger) fail to finish. Cheetah (G601) is the first Swiss marque to participate. André Haller, a restauranteur from Strasbourg is killed (Datsun 240Z) on Mulsanne Straight.

1977 Alpine-Renault launch first major attempt to win but all three fail with engine problems. Porsche triumphs despite a piston failing in the last hour - it crawled round to win! Inaltera wins GTP category. First appearance of the Swiss marque Sauber. Chevron B36 wins its class (using Simca/Chrysler motor).

978 Alpine-Renault versus Porsche - the French car wins (Jaussaud/Pironi) and Renault retires from sports-car racing to concentrate on Formula 1. Ferrari 512 BB begins its six year career at Le Mans.

979 "Works" Porsches fail and victory goes to the Kremer Porsche 935 K3 (Ludwig/Whittington brothers) in wet race. First win for a rear-engined car. WM has its first success by winning GTP class. First appearance of the unusual Dome Zeros which retire.

980 First win for driver/constructor (Rondeau-Jaussaud/Rondeau). Lancia reappears officially with Beta Monte Carlos. Porsche concentrates on three "works" 924 GTs. WM 4th, its best result.

981 Porsche back on top (Ickx/Bell), the Belgian now with a record-breaking five wins at Le Mans. We can call this victory the start of the First German Period in Le Mans history. A Ferrari 512 BB wins its category. Boutsen has a serious accident near Mulsanne in the WM, killing a marshal and bringing out the "pace car" for the first time in Le Mans history. Jean-Louis Lafosse (Rondeau) killed on Mulsanne Straight.

982 Le Mans adopts the new Group C regulations (accent on fuel consumption). 16 of the 29 entries in Group C used Ford-Cosworth engine (including two Zakspeed entered Ford C 100s). No Ford revival nor Aston Martin (with the new Nimrod). New Porsche 956 (to become the most successful Le Mans car ever) took the first three places, giving Ickx his sixth (record) win. IMSA Chevrolet Camaro finishes (17th).

983 Porsche built customer 956s for 1983 and, together with "works" cars, these filled the first eight places. Winning car of Schuppan/Haywood/Holbert only just made it to finish with engine overheating! Mazda wins Group C Junior.

984 No "works" Porsches in protest at FISA's change of rules. Joest private 956 (Ludwig/Pescarolo) wins, with similar cars in first seven places. American Group-44 Jaguars appear. Serious accident involving two Aston-Martin Nimrods on Mulsanne Straight-marshal killed. Last appearance of a Ferrari at Le Mans until 1994. Works Lancia LC2 in lead for nine hours. BMW M1 wins Group B class, and Lola-Mazda (T616) Group C2.

1985   Same Joest car (956-117) wins again as works Porsches (962C) struggle with problematical engine management systems. Tiga wins Group C2 and the Jaguar XJR5 the IMSA GTP class. Nielsen (Sauber-Mercedes) becomes airborn on Mulsanne Straight during practice.

1986   New Mulsanne corner (with section to by-pass the new roundabout) inaugurated in the preliminary trials in May. Porsche 961 is the first four-wheel drive car to participate and wins IMSA GTX class. "Works" Porsche 962C (Bell/Holbert/Stuck) wins. TWR Jaguars appear but retire as do the Sauber-Mercedes. ADA-run Gebhardt wins C2 Class. Fatal accident to Austrian Jo Gartner (Porsche 962C) at night on Mulsanne Straight.

1987   New chicane incorporated in the Dunlop curve after the pits. Porsche (Bell/Holbert/Stuck) defeats Jaguar. Cougar-Porsche finishes 3rd. Spice wins C2.

1988   April/May preliminary trials cancelled. WM-Peugeot (Dorchy) achieves 405 k.p.h. on Mulsanne Straight. TWR Jaguar (Wallace/Lammers/Dumfries) beats off determined Porsche threat. Sauber-Mercedes withdraw before start because of tyre trouble. Spice C2 winner.

1989   Silver Sauber-Mercedes C9s take first two places. Several cars victims of spectacular fires. Aston Martin returns (11th). Cougar wins C2.

1990   Two chicanes inserted in Mulsanne Straight. Jaguar's seventh victory (Brundle/Nielsen/Cobb). Big effort by Nissan to win with Lola-based cars. Spice wins C2 and Mazda IMSA GTP.

1991   New pits and race control complex replaces those built in 1956. First win for a Japanese car (Mazda) and first for a rotary-engined car. Official return of Peugeot (two 905s). Sauber-Mercedes team led four-fifths of the race but encountered engine problems. Michael Schumacher's only participation - he finished 5th. Jaguar XJR-14s did not start. Last appearance of a Lancia.

1992   Crisis in sports-car racing - only 28 starters. First win for Peugeot and first for a V-10 motor. Mazda came 4th with a Jaguar XJR-14 based Judd-engined car! Big Toyota effort with TS 010 2nd and 8th.

1993   Return of GT cars to Le Mans. Preliminary trials re-instated. Peugeot score 1-2-3. W.R. first to win a category with a central driving position. Runners included Venturis, Lotus Esprits, Jaguar XJ220Cs, one of which won the GT category only to be disqualified later.

994 Jochen Dauer "converts" his Porsche 962s into GT versions, conforms to the regulations if not the spirit and wins (Baldi/Dalmas/Haywood)! This begins the Second German Period in Le Mans history.

995 McLaren wins on first appearance, albeit with a German V-12 BMW engine! First overall victory for a car with a central driving position.

996 Joest-entered TWR Porsche victory (Jones/Reuter/Wurz), Wurz at 22 the youngest ever winner.

997 The same TWR Porsche (chassis WSC 001) wins again (Alboreto/Johansson/Kristensen). Leading "works" Porsche 911 GT1 caught fire with just over two hours to go. Gulf McLarens also victims of fire, one in practice, one in final stages of race when 5th. Porsche wins GT2. First appearance of the Panoz GTR1 - all four retired, one after catching fire. Serious effort to win by Nissan with the R390 - they could only salvage a 12th place.

998 Toyota and Mercedes take on Porsche, the latter overcoming strong opposition for its 16th win (McNish/Ortelli/Aiello in 911 GT1 98). Mercedes (CLK LM) both fail early on as do "works" BMWs. Toyota's GT-One could only manage 9th. Oreca Chrysler Viper wins GT2. Fine 4th place by private McLaren (O'Rourke, Sugden and Auberlen). Nissan takes 3rd, 5th, 6th and 10th.

999 First 100% win for BMW. Mercedes CLRs take off vertically in practice and, after Dumbreck's similar fate in the race, are withdrawn. Launch of the American Le Mans series (A.C.O. and Donald Panoz). First appearance of Audi which finish 3rd and 4th. Toyota GT-One comes second. Oreca Viper again wins its class (LM GTS).

000 First win for Audi which takes first three places. Revival of American interest with Cadillac, Chevrolet, and Chrysler engines in Reynards. Pescarolo's private Courage - Peugeot finishes a fine 4th. Panoz roadsters manage 5th, 6th. Disappointing Cadillacs, one on fire early on! Oreca Chrysler Viper wins GTS, a hat-trick. Lola (B2K/40) wins LMP 675 class. First involvement of Volkswagen at Le Mans (engine for the ROC - Reynards).

2001 Hump at end of Mulsanne Straight flattened. Audi 1-2 with same winning drivers (Biela-Kristensen-Pirro). Bentley (with Audi motor) 3rd, its team-mate retired after fire. Corvette wins its class (LM GTS), 8th overall, still the marque's highest finish since 1960. Reynard-Volkswagen wins LMP 675 and finishes an excellent 5th overall. Rain storm unexpectedly at Arnage on the 4th lap causes an accident that eliminates several cars including first-timer Pilbeam. Very wet race causes many retirements. Oreca run Chrysler scores 4th, one of the cars retiring with engine trouble the other catching fire on Mulsanne Straight. Re-appearance of Dome, M.G. (Ex 257) and Callaway. Début of Ascari marque.

2002 New sweeping section down to the Esses used for the first time in May preliminary trials. Audi triumphs for third successive year and a historical first: all three drivers score a hat-trick of wins (Biela, Kristensen, Pirro). Dry hot race produces surprisingly similar results to previous year's wet race: Bentley best of the rest and GTP winner, Corvettes win GTS and Porsche the GT class. Dramatic win in last five minutes for Reynard-Volkswagen in P675 class as the WR limps across the line on three wheels following a rear suspension failure! Cadillacs off the pace, M.G. Lolas shine in early stages but retire; American-entered M.G. Lola caught fire during the night on Mulsanne Straight (first chicane). All Ferraris retired as did the Morgan Aero 8 on marque's first appearance for 40 years.

Le Mans Statistics

Year	Winning car	Drivers	Distance (km)	Average (kph)
1923	Chenard & Walcker	Lagache/Léonard	2209,536	92,06
1924	Bentley	Duff/Clement	2077,340	86,555
1925	La Lorraine	de Courcelles/Rossignol	2233,982	93,082
1926	La Lorraine	Bloch/Rossignol	2552,414	106,350
1927	Bentley	Dr. Benjafield/Davis	2369,807	98,740
1928	Bentley	Barnato/Rubin	2669,272	111,219
1929	Bentley	Barnato/Birkin	2843,830	118,492
1930	Bentley	Barnato/Kidston	2930,663	122,111
1931	Alfa Romeo	Lord Howe/Birkin	3017,654	125,735
1932	Alfa Romeo	Sommer/Chinetti	2954,038	123,084
1933	Alfa Romeo	Nuvolari/Sommer	3144,038	131,001
1934	Alfa Romeo	Chinetti/Etancelin	2886,938	120,289
1935	Lagonda	Hindmarsh/Fontes	3006,797	125,283
1937	Bugatti	Wimille/Benoist	3287,938	136,997
1938	Delahaye	Chaboud/Tremoulet	3180,940	132,539
1939	Bugatti	Wimille/Veyron	3354,760	139,781
1949	Ferrari	Lord Selsdon/Chinetti	3178,299	132,420
1950	Talbot	Rosier/Rosier	3465,120	144,380
1951	Jaguar	Walker/Whitehead	3611,193	150,466
1952	Mercedes	Lang/Reiss	3733,800	155,575
1953	Jaguar	Rolt/Hamilton	4088,064	170,336
1954	Ferrari	Gonzales/Trintignant	4061,150	169,215
1955	Jaguar	Hawthorn/Bueb	4135,380	172,308
1956	Jaguar	Flockhart/Sanderson	4034,929	168,122
1957	Jaguar	Flockhart/Bueb	4397,108	183,217
1958	Ferrari	P. Hill/Gendebien	4101,926	170,914
1959	AstonMartin	Salvadori/Shelby	4347,900	181,163
1960	Ferrari	Frère/Gendebien	4217,527	175,730
1961	Ferrari	Gendebien/P.Hill	4476,580	186,527
1962	Ferrari	Gendebien/P.Hill	4451,255	185,469
1963	Ferrari	Scarfiotti/Bandini	4561,710	190,071
1964	Ferrari	Guichet/Vaccarella	4695,310	195,638

Year	Winning car	Drivers	Distance (km)	Average (kph)
1965	Ferrari	Gregory/Rindt	4677,110	194,880
1966	Ford	Amon/McLaren	4843,090	201,795
1967	Ford	Gurney/Foyt	5232,900	218,038
1968	Ford	Rodriguez/Bianchi	4452,880	185,536
1969	Ford	Ickx/Oliver	4998,000	208,250
1970	Porsche	Attwood/Herrmann	4607,810	191,992
1971	Porsche	Marko/van Lennep	5335,313	222,304
1972	Matra	Pescarolo/G. Hill	4691,343	195,472
1973	Matra	Pescarolo/Larrousse	4853,945	202,247
1974	Matra	Pescarolo/Larrousse	4606,571	191,940
1975	Gulf-Ford	Ickx/Bell	4595,577	191,482
1976	Porsche	Ickx/van Lennep	4769,923	198,746
1977	Porsche	Barth/Haywood/Ickx	4671,630	194,651
1978	Renault	Pironi/Jaussaud	5044,530	210,188
1979	Porsche	Ludwig/Whittington /Whittington	4173,930	173,913
1980	Rondeau	Rondeau/Jaussaud	4608,020	192,000
1981	Porsche	Ickx/Bell	4825,348	201,056
1982	Porsche	Ickx/Bell	4899,086	204,128
1983	Porsche	Holbert/Haywood/Schuppan	5047,934	210,330
1984	Porsche	Pescarolo/Ludwig	4900,276	204,178
1985	Porsche	Ludwig/Barilla/"Winter"	5088,507	212,021
1986	Porsche	Stuck/Bell/Holbert	4972,731	207,197
1987	Porsche	Stuck/Bell/Holbert	4791,777	199,657
1988	Jaguar	Lammers/Dumfries/Wallace	5332,790	221,665
1989	Sauber-Mercedes	Mass/Dickens/Reuter	5265,115	219,990
1990	Jaguar	Brundle/Nielsen/Cobb	4882,400	204,036
1991	Mazda	Weidler/Herbert/Gachot	4922,810	205,333
1992	Peugeot	Warwick/Dalmas/Blundell	4787,200	199,340
1993	Peugeot	Brabham/Bouchut/Helary	5100,000	213,358
1994	Porsche	Dalmas/Haywood/Baldi	4685,701	195,238
1995	McLaren-BMW	Dalmas/Lehto/Sekiya	4055,800	168,992
1996	Porsche	Reuter/Jones/Wurz	4814,400	200,600
1997	Porsche	Alboreto/Johansson /Kristensen	4909,600	204,186
1998	Porsche	Aiello/Ortelli/McNish	4783,781	199,324
1999	BMW	Winkelhock/Martini/Dalmas	4967,991	207,624
2000	Audi	Biela/Kristensen/Pirro	5007,988	208,666
2001	Audi	Biela/Kristensen/Pirro	4367,200	180,949
2002	Audi	Biela/Kristensen/Pirro	5118,750	213,068

Index of Performance

Year	Winning Car
1926	O.M.
1927	Salmson
1928	Salmson
1929	Bentley
1930	Talbot
1931	Alfa-Romeo
1932	Alfa-Romeo
1933	Riley
1934	Riley
1935	Aston Martin
1937	Bugatti
1938	Simca
1939	Simca
1949	Ferrari
1950	Monopole, Aston Martin
1951	Monopole
1952	Monopole
1953	Panhard
1954	D.B.
1955	Porsche
1956	D.B.
1957	Lotus
1958	OSCA
1959	D.B.
1960	D.B.
1961	D.B.
1962	Panhard
1963	Ferrari
1964	Ferrari
1965	Porsche
1966	Porsche
1967	Porsche
1968	Alpine
1969	Alpine
1970	Porsche
1971	Porsche

Index of Thermal Efficiency

Year	Winning Car
1959	D.B.
1960	Lotus
1961	Sunbeam
1962	Lotus
1963	René-Bonnet
1964	Alpine
1965	Porsche
1966	Alpine
1967	Ford
1968	Alpine
1969	Ford
1970	Porsche
1971	Ferrari
1972	Ferrari
1973	Porsche
1974	Ferrari